I-DRIVE
The Holy Land Experience
The Mall at Millenia
Orlando Premium Outlets-International Drive
Fun Spot America Orlando
Rebounderz
TANGELO PARK
Eaglewood Golf Course
Shingle Creek Golf Club
Aquatica
Faldo Golf Institute
OAK RIDGE ROAD WEST
SAND LAKE ROAD WEST
LANDSTREET ROAD WEST
FLORIDA'S TURNPIKE
METRO ORLANDO
500 m
500 yds
DubsDread Golf Course
WINTER PARK
Lake Virginia
Mead Botanical Gardens
Lake Silver
Lake Sue
Orlando Science Center
Loch Haven Park
Orlando Museum of Art
Mennello Museum of American Art
Harry P Leu Gardens
COLLEGE PARK
PRINCETOWN STREET WEST
Antique Row
Orlando Country Club & Golf Course
COLONIAL DRIVE WEST
COLONIAL DRIVE EAST
Eola Park
Thornton Park
Orange County Regional History Center
Orlando Festival Park
SOUTH STREET EAST
EAST-WEST EXPRESSWAY
ANDERSON STREET EAST
ORANGE BLOSSOM TRAIL NORTH
EDGEWATER DRIVE
ORANGE AVENUE NORTH
MILLS AVENUE NORTH

Fodor's

25 Best

ORLANDO

WITH UNIVERSAL®, SEAWORLD®, WALT DISNEY WORLD®

How to Use This Book

KEY TO SYMBOLS

- Map reference to the accompanying fold-out map
- Address
- Telephone number
- Opening/closing times
- Restaurant or café
- Nearest rail station
- Nearest subway (Metro) station
- Nearest bus route
- Nearest riverboat or ferry stop
- Facilities for visitors with disabilities
- Other practical information
- Further information
- Tourist information
- Admission charges: Very expensive (over $50), Expensive ($25–$50), Moderate ($10–$50) and Inexpensive ($10 or less)

This guide is divided into four sections

• Essential Orlando: An introduction to the city and tips on making the most of your stay.

• Orlando by Area: We've broken the city into five areas, and recommended the best sights, shops, entertainment venues, nightlife and restaurants in each one. Suggested walks help you to explore on foot.

• Where to Stay: The best hotels, whether you're looking for luxury, budget or something in between.

• Need to Know: The info you need to make your trip run smoothly, including getting about by public transportation, weather tips, emergency phone numbers and useful websites.

Navigation In the Orlando by Area chapter, we've given each area its own color, which is also used on the locator maps throughout the book and the map on the inside front cover.

Maps The fold-out map accompanying this book is a comprehensive street plan of Orlando. The grid on this fold-out map is the same as the grid on the locator maps within the book. We've given grid references within the book for each sight and listing.

Contents

Introducing Orlando

Say Orlando and most people think theme park. Disney and Universal pleasure palaces have really put this city on the world map. But look beyond the obvious and you may be surprised by what else you find.

Orlando isn't so much a place as a portal. Dive headlong into Tomorrowland or trek backward through time to Jurassic Park. It's a city of Lands created with such precision that we forget our everyday lives—whatever our age. The city thrives on "the wow factor"—fastest, highest, deepest, longest. An attraction doesn't even make it on to the tourist "must do" detector if it doesn't come with its own superlative, or preferably a string of them.

Unlike in many destinations, people are pretty sure what they are arriving in Orlando for. They expect to have fun; nothing too cerebral, no heavy culture, just unadulterated pleasure. And the city works hard to make fun seem effortless.

With the magnetic pull of the theme parks so strong, it's amazing that the rest of the city manages any visibility at all, but there is life beyond the shadow of the "ears." Orlando is a lively city and the social hub of central Florida. With resident ballet and orchestral companies, plus some well-respected museum collections, it enjoys a vibrant arts scene.

Thornton Park and Winter Park are the city's most picturesque and enchanting residential neighborhoods. Urbanites living here have tree-lined avenues, painted picket fences and porches on which to spend balmy evenings; plus a great café society.

Orlando's parks have enough thrills to fill several vacations and they certainly keep the city economically buoyant; however, the razzmatazz and fairy dust are only one part of the story of this Florida city.

Facts + Figures

- **57.1 million visitors (2012)**
- **More than 100 attractions**
- **116,000 hotel rooms**
- **5,300 restaurants**
- **Over 100 nightlife venues**
- **33 percent of jobs in the city are related directly to tourism**

GETTING DOWN TO BUSINESS

Orlando's Orange County Convention Center, on the bustling 5-mile-long (8km) International Drive, is the second largest in the United States with 2.1 million sq ft (195,000 sq m) of exhibition space. The city welcomes over 5 million convention visitors every year, with everyone from surgeons to pet food purveyors getting together for their industry powwow.

© Disney

GREEN ROOTS

It's still possible to find an unspoiled natural Orlando, remote from the artificial 21st-century pleasures. Ruled by water, this landscape is thousands of years old and supports a complicated and sensitive ecosystem where three animals reign supreme. No, not Mickey, Donald and Goofy, but the brown bear, the Florida cougar and the American alligator.

HISTORY RECALLED

Orlando is the capital of Orange County, named for the crop that made Florida rich a century ago. The names of the two other counties in the area pay homage to the Native American tribes living here in earlier eras of history. Seminole County remembers the Seminoles, while Osceola remembers the brave but defeated leader of the Seminoles.

A Short Stay in Orlando

DAY 1

Morning Breakfast with the world's most famous rodent, Mickey Mouse, at **Chef Mickey's** (▷ 43), to set you up for your action-packed day. Then get to **Magic Kingdom®** (▷ 28–29) as the gates open to make the most of your time and take a daily activity sheet to tell you when the parades and character appearances will be. Start with **Space Mountain®** (▷ 39), then wander to **Fantasyland** (▷ 37) to enjoy The Many Adventures of Winnie the Pooh and Peter Pan's Flight.

Mid-morning Move on to **Adventureland** (▷ 28) to try Pirates of the Caribbean, some aspects of which may be a bit too scary for younger children.

Lunch Dine with royalty as a collection of Disney princesses arrive for lunch at **Cinderella's Royal Table** in Cinderella Castle (▷ 43).

© Disney

© Disney

Afternoon Retrace your steps around the park, taking in the rides you missed earlier. These include Mickey's PhilharMagic, Splash Mountain®, Jungle Cruise and—wait for your lunch to settle—**Big Thunder Mountain Railroad** (▷ 36).

Mid-afternoon Don't forget to be in place on **Main Street USA®** (▷ 39) for the afternoon parade (usually starting at 3pm).

Dinner Fine dine at **Artist Point** (▷ 43) or enjoy the fun of **Bongo's Cuban Café™** (▷ 43).

Evening Take in the **Cirque du Soleil®–La Nouba™** show (▷ 37) at **Downtown Disney®/Disney Springs** (▷ 27), then drop into Raglan Road Irish Pub to enjoy the live band and perhaps a pint of Guinness.

© Disney

© Disney

© *La Nouba* by Cirque du Soleil®

© *La Nouba* by Cirque du Soleil®

DAY 2

Morning Be ready to join the early birds as **Universal Studios®** (▷ 48–49) opens and head first for the far side of the park to the thrills and scares of **Revenge of the Mummy™** (▷ 55). Then move on to **TRANSFORMERS: The Ride-3D** (▷ 49).

Mid-morning Head for **The Simpsons Ride™** (▷ 49) before moving next door to **Men in Black™ Alien Attack™** (▷ 55).

Lunch For a full-service meal, eat at **Lombard's Seafood Grille** (▷ 58) at Lombard's Landing; for snacks, **Mel's Drive In** (▷ 58) is the place to go.

Afternoon Let your meal settle while enjoying **Shrek 4-D™** (▷ 55). Next you'll want to do the other major attractions based on Universal box-office movie hits. The cyborg rampages through Earth in **TERMINATOR 2®: 3-D** (▷ 55), your gentle boat ride becomes a fight against a man-eating watery predator in **Jaws®** (▷ 49) and on **TWISTER...Ride It Out®** (▷ 49) you'll see the havoc a tornado can cause.

Mid-afternoon The final ride you may want to undertake is the seriously scary **Hollywood Rip Ride Rockit®** (▷ 54), the tallest coaster in the city, reaching an eye-watering 17 stories above ground level.

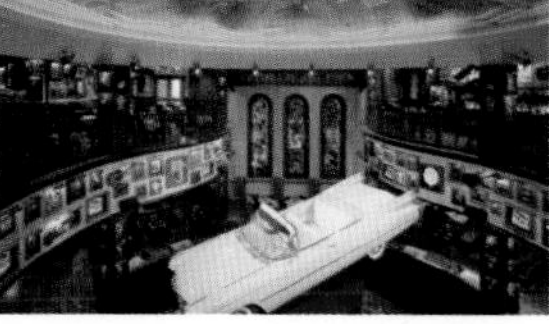

Dinner Try a fantastic steak at **Palm** (▷ 58), or dine casual at **Hard Rock Café** (▷ 58).

Evening Stroll the venues at **CityWalk®** (▷ 53), Universal's entertainment complex. There are plenty of choices here for an after-dinner drink, featuring all manner of musical styles and live performances. Alternatively, you can take in a movie or head to a club—the sky's the limit.

Top 25

Boggy Creek Airboat Rides ▷ 92 Spot the crocodile on a thrilling airboat ride across the swamps.

Celebration ▷ 26 New yet old-fashioned, this planned town is a relaxing place to spend a few hours.

Central Florida Zoo ▷ 93 A collection of Florida's native creatures in their own habitat.

Wonderworks ▷ 66 An eye-catching attraction with interactive games, old and new, and virtual reality experiences.

Winter Park ▷ 82 A delightful excursion away from the theme parks, with excellent shopping.

Wekiwa Springs State Park ▷ 95 Few places in Orlando match up to this park's natural beauty.

Universal Studios Islands of Adventure® ▷ 50–51 A larger-than-life, primary-colored cartoon world with all the old favorites.

Universal Studios® ▷ 48–49 Exhilarating rides, magical shows and other attractions re-create the movie magic.

Universal CityWalk® ▷ 53 This huge entertainment complex is home to clubs, restaurants and stores.

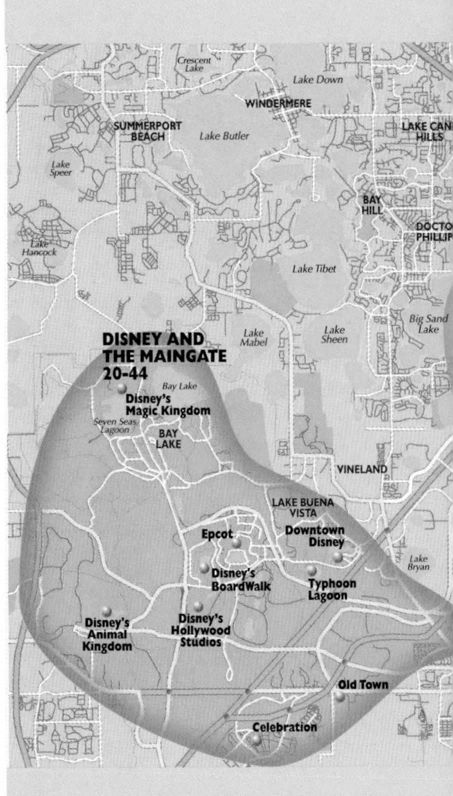

Typhoon Lagoon ▷ 35 Fun water park that re-creates Florida's ocean and sandy white beaches.

SeaWorld ▷ 64–65 One of the world's largest and most popular marine-life parks.

Pointe Orlando ▷ 63 International Drive's dining, shopping and entertainment hub.

These pages are a quick guide to the Top 25, which are described in more detail later. Here they are listed alphabetically, and the tinted background shows which area they are in.

Discovery Cove ▷ 62 A day's worth of marine encounters where you can swim with dolphins.

Disney's Animal Kingdom® ▷ 24 This is another world—there's no doubt about it.

Disney's BoardWalk ▷ 25 Entertainment, shopping and eating in a 1930s East Coast setting.

Disney's Hollywood Studios ▷ 30–31 A celebration of the movies with Mickey Mouse and friends.

Disney's Magic Kingdom® ▷ 28–29 Disney's showcase, which put Florida on the map, still draws the crowds.

Downtown Disney® ▷ 27 Shopping, dining and entertainment that takes in three districts.

Epcot® ▷ 32–33 A showcase for technology and science, and a window on the world.

Gatorland ▷ 94 Pens and pools teeming with alligators and daily shows.

Harry P. Leu Gardens ▷ 78 Acres of lush gardens in the heart of Orlando.

Old Town ▷ 34 Take a trip back in time to join the mods and rockers in 1950s downtown USA.

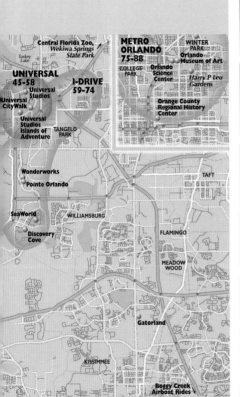

Orlando Science Center ▷ 81 A complex crowned by an observatory and anchored by the CineDome.

Orlando Museum of Art ▷ 80 See the work of nationally and world-renowned artists.

Orange County Regional History Center ▷ 79 Find out what Orlando was like before the mouse.

Shopping

Shopping is listed as the number one activity for international visitors to Orlando, even scoring above the world-beating attractions. And retail therapy also attracts domestic visitors to the city, with 45 percent spending time spending cash. And here Orlando beats the competition again: It's one of the primary shopping cities in the country, with over 73 million sq ft (6.78 million sq m) of retail space, and it's still growing.

More for your Money

The classic styling, good quality and exceptional value of American brand products make shopping for clothing and household items, particularly good value. For clothing, fashionable brands such as Tommy Hilfiger, Calvin Klein, DKNY, Levi's and Timberland are the names to watch for.

Outlet Stores

Orlando is particularly famed for its "outlet" stores, where designer and mainstream brands sell end-of-line or seasonal items and lower-quality products at a discounted rate (savings of up to 70 percent on the American store price). Some of the merchandise are seconds or flawed items but if you don't mind that you get a great deal. Hundreds of thousands of square feet of retail space is devoted to low-cost shopping, with stores conveniently gathered together in specialist shopping malls.

From character merchandise to designer labels—it's shop 'til you drop in Orlando

SOMETHING OLD

American collectibles form a small but interesting section of the Orlando shopping market. Genuine antiques date from the late 19th century, just before the coming of mass production, and include pottery, glassware and original quilts and soft furnishings. Many portable items are hand-made and often bear the initials or name of the original owner and the date they were made, making for a really personal souvenir.

Something Different

Though the city's predominant shopping environment for good-quality, mass-produced consumer goods is the shopping mall, Orlando offers several farmers' markets and arts festivals throughout the year where you can buy one-of-a-kind arts-and-crafts items. The downtown core, Winter Park and Celebration are the most favored locations.

Theme Park Souvenirs

No one should end a trip to Orlando without a souvenir of their favorite character, be it Spider-Man, Shamu, Shrek or Harry Potter. All the parks have excellent on-site shopping where you can buy bona fide souvenirs from the glitzy to the kitsch, such as original and unique hand-drawn celluloid cartoon fiches to fridge magnets. Character-embossed T-shirts and baseball caps are sold by the millions and are especially practical in the hot Florida climate. Although there's something for every budget, prices are high. Quality is rigorously controlled and the elaborate and inventive store designs make shopping a real pleasure: Disney and Universal take as much care over store design as they do over their rides and shows. Outside the park boundaries, other souvenir shops also cash in on the popularity of the theme parks, but these will not be officially endorsed goods so beware of quality differences.

SHOP THE WORLD

Epcot's World Showcase at Walt Disney World is a fantastic place to buy goods from around the world, from the exotic to the mundane, without needing to use your passport. Choose from colorful cotton blankets and sombreros from Mexico; pure wool sweaters and toboggans from Norway; Steiff Teddy bears and ceramic beer steins from Germany; sheepskin bags and leather belts from Morocco; Limoge porcelain and Bordeaux wine from France; tea and tea sets from the United Kingdom; jade and silk from China; Venetian glass from Italy and maple syrup from Canada.

Shopping by Theme

Whether you're looking for an outlet store, a quirky boutique, or something in between, you'll find it all in Orlando. On this page shops are listed by theme. For a more detailed write-up, see the individual listings in Orlando by Area.

COLLECTIBLES

A&T Antiques (▷86)
The Black Sheep (▷86)
The City Arts Factory (▷86)
Custom Tag Shop (▷40)
Orlando Harley-Davidson (▷105)
Scott Laurent Collection (▷86)
Sheplers Western Store (▷71)
Tharoo & Co (▷71)
Timothy's Gallery (▷86)

DESIGNER LABELS

Ax Armani Exchange (▷70)
Chanel (▷70)
Gucci (▷70)
Jimmy Choo (▷70)
Oakley (▷105)
Off 5th–Saks Fifth Avenue Outlet (▷71)
Polo Ralph Lauren Factory Store (▷71)
Zou Zou Boutique (▷86)

FOR SPORTS FANS

Bass Pro Shops Outdoor World (▷70)
Edwin Watts Golf (▷70)
Foot Locker (▷70)
Nike (▷70)
Teva (▷71)

FROM OVERSEAS

The Brass Bazaar (▷40)
Souvenirs de France (▷40)

HOUSEHOLD GOODS

Williams-Sonoma (▷86)

MAINSTREAM BRANDS

Bass & Co (▷70)
Guess (▷105)
Levi's® Outlet Store (▷70)
Nine West (▷105)
Timberland (▷71)
Tommy Bahama Emporium (▷71)
Tommy Hilfiger (▷71)
Victoria's Secret (▷105)

MICKEY AND FRIENDS

Art of Disney (▷40)
The Big Shop (▷105)
Disney Pin Traders (▷40)
Disney's Wonderful World of Memories (▷40)
Emporium (▷40)
Stage 1 Company Store (▷40)
World of Disney Stores® (▷40)

THEMED MERCHANDISE

Endangered Species Store® (▷56)
Gatorland (▷105)
Kennedy Space Center (▷105)
Leu Gardens (▷86)
Medieval Times (▷105)
Morse Museum (▷86)
La Nouba (▷40)
Orlando Museum of Art (▷86)
Orlando Science Center (▷86)

UNIVERSAL SOUVENIRS

All the Books You Can Read (▷56)
Comic Book Shop (▷56)
Dervish & Banges® (▷56)
Dinostore℠ (▷56)
Disney Character Warehouse (▷70)
The Marvel Alterniverse Store® (▷56)
MIB Gear (▷56)
Supply Vault (▷56)
Universal Studios Store® (▷56)

Orlando by Night

Neon glitz and glamor from International Drive to CityWalk—you'll never be short of something to do

The fun doesn't stop once the theme parks close, and as soon as you've seen the obligatory fireworks extravaganza you can start your evening entertainment.

Theme Party

But that does not mean leaving the main theme parks. Universal in particular offers an excellent range of live music with local, national and international headline acts, clubs with resident and guest DJs, and comedy clubs. Family fun also continues after dark. Dinner shows are a staple of Orlando's holiday scene and if you want to fight with pirates, joust with knights and cheer the hero these are all enjoyable, well-choreographed events. International Drive is also a hub of activities, with nightclubs and bars in the large hotel complexes around the convention center.

Downtown

If you want to mingle with Orlando's suburbanites, head for downtown. On sultry summer evenings Wall Street Plaza has a buzzing atmosphere. Church Street's clubs and The Amway Center are within walking distance, while a short taxi ride away you can stroll through Thornton Park, with its chic eateries. Orlando is the cultural core of central Florida and offers a good program of ballet, opera and concerts. The theaters at Loch Haven are the major venues, and the Dr. Phillips Center for the Performing Arts opens its doors in late 2014.

AN EVENING STROLL

As the sun sets, 1,000 neon lights illuminate Orlando. The strip around Pointe Orlando along International Drive and the evening venues of Disney and Universal are great locations for a stroll among the "bright lights," while Thornton Park and Winter Park are smarter neighborhoods with limited neon but great eateries and cafés. However, not all neighborhoods are as safe as these. We would recommend taking transportation to most evening venues.

Eating Out

Eating out is one of the great pleasures of a trip to Orlando. You can just about get what you want when you want it, and you'll never be far away from delicious food, whatever your budget.

All Cuisines, All Day

Whether it's a simple snack, a specific cuisine –Italian or Chinese for instance—or an all-you-can-eat buffet, you'll find it here. Service starts at breakfast and often runs continuously through to late evening.

Take a Break

The major theme parks all cater to their guests very well, with a range of simple café-type venues, from a quick pit-stop between attractions to full-service restaurants.

Choice for Kids

Orlando restaurants are very family friendly so your children will get a warm welcome and, usually, their own special menus. A meal with Mickey, Spider-Man or other famous friends will make their trip extra special.

First-class Dining

Orlando has built up quite a reputation for quality dining in recent years. Several renowned chefs have brought their menus here, so you are spoiled for choice if you want to book a romantic gourmet dinner. You'll need to book tables well in advance at these select venues.

RESTAURANTS: DID YOU KNOW?

According to research compiled by the American Restaurant Association in 2013:
There were 990,000 restaurants in the USA.
Restaurants took $1.8 billion in sales every day.
For every $100 spent on food in the USA, $47 was spent in restaurants.
Half of all Americans have worked in a restaurant at some stage during their lives, and 13.5 million Americans currently work in restaurants.

Eating Orlando style—alfresco, theme dining or just good old-fashioned home cooking

Restaurants by Cuisine

There are restaurants to suit all tastes and budgets in Orlando. On this page they are listed by cuisine. For a more detailed description of each restaurant, see Orlando by Area.

AMERICAN STAPLES

Bahama Breeze (▷ 73)
The Cheesecake Factory (▷ 73)
Keke's (▷ 74)
Olive Garden (▷ 74)
Rainforest Café® (▷ 44)

CELEBRITY LINKS

Bongo's Cuban Café™ (▷ 43)
Hard Rock Cafe (▷ 58)
Jimmy Buffet's® Margaritaville® (▷ 58)
NASCAR® Sports Grille (▷ 58)
Planet Hollywood (▷ 44)

CHARACTER DINING

1900 Park Fare (▷ 43)
Chef Mickey's (▷ 43)
Cinderella's Royal Table (▷ 43)
Crystal Palace at Main Street (▷ 43)
Dine with an Astronaut (▷ 106)
Garden Grill (▷ 44)
Liberty Tree Tavern (▷ 44)

EUROPEAN

Brio Tuscan Grille and Bakery (▷ 88)
Ceviche (▷ 88)
Citrico's (▷ 43)
Columbia Restaurant (▷ 43)
Primo (▷ 106)
The Ravenous Pig (▷ 88)
Restaurant Marrakesh (▷ 44)
Taverna Opa (▷ 74)

FANTASTIC FUSION

Café Tu Tu Tango (▷ 73)
Emeril's Tchoup Chop (▷ 58)
Mythos Restaurant (▷ 58)
Roy's (▷ 74)

FAST FOOD

Austin's Coffee (▷ 88)
B-Line Diner (▷ 73)
Bubbalou's Bodacious Bar-B-Que (▷ 88)
Crispers (▷ 106)
Dave & Buster's (▷ 73)
Dexters (▷ 88)
Earl of Sandwich (▷ 43)
Johnny Rockets (▷ 74)
Mel's Drive In (▷ 58)
The Sci-Fi Dine-In Theater Restaurant (▷ 44)
Sonic (▷ 74)

FRESH FLAVORS

Greens & Grille (▷ 74)
Kouzzina by Cat Cora® (▷ 44)
Luma on Park (▷ 88)
Seasons 52 (▷ 106)

GOURMET EXPERIENCE

Artist Point (▷ 43)
Bluezoo (▷ 43)
La Boheme (▷ 88)
The Capital Grille (▷ 73)
Norman's (▷ 106)
Victoria and Albert's (▷ 44)

SURF AND TURF

Charley's Steak House (▷ 73)
Fishbones (▷ 73)
Fulton's Crab House (▷ 44)
Kres (▷ 88)
Lombard's Seafood Grille (▷ 58)
Palm (▷ 58)
Red Lobster (▷ 74)
Texas de Brazil (▷ 74)

TABLE WITH A VIEW

Dine with Shamu® (▷ 73)
Hillstone (▷ 88)

TASTE OF THE EAST

Kimono's (▷ 44)
Thai Thani (▷ 74)

Top Tips For...

However you'd like to spend your time in Orlando, these top suggestions should help you tailor your ideal visit. Each sight or listing has a fuller write-up elsewhere in the book.

A GOURMET EXPERIENCE

Sample Emeril Lagasse's Cajun creations at Emeril's (▷ 58).
Taste the finest New World cuisine at Norman's (▷ 106), the restaurant of Norman van Aken.
Enjoy award-winning menus at Victoria and Albert's (▷ 44).

ADRENALIN RUSHES

Don't split your shirt on the Incredible Hulk Coaster® (▷ 54).
Hold on tight on Big Thunder Mountain Railroad (▷ 36).
Don't lose the thread at the Amazing Adventures of Spider-Man® (▷ 54).

Don't eat too much before you go on that ride

ANIMAL ENCOUNTERS

Wrestle with a croc, under expert guidance, at Gatorland (▷ 94).
Swim with the dolphins at Discovery Cove (▷ 62).
See Florida's animals in the wild with Boggy Creek Airboat Rides (▷ 92).

DINING WITH MICKEY AND FRIENDS

The world's most famous mouse invites you to breakfast or dinner at Chef Mickey's (▷ 43).
Take dinner with Cinderella and her friends during Cinderella's Happily Ever After Dinner (▷ 43).
Start the day with Pooh and friends at Crystal Palace at Main Street (▷ 43).

Boggy Creek airboat ride; animals feature in many experiences on a trip to Orlando

Life is full of fantasy and neon lights

© Disney

KICKS FOR KIDS

Enter the realms of fantasy at Universal Studios Islands of Adventure® (▷ 50–51).

Give the little ones a go on the gentler rides at Fantasyland (▷ 37) where they can meet Snow White, Dumbo or Peter Pan.

Take a tour of Kid's Town at Orlando Science Center (▷ 81).

FREE STUFF

Peruse the galleries at Cornell Museum of Fine Arts (▷ 82).

Rev your engines at the automobile and bike parades at Old Town (▷ 34).

Take in the panorama of neon on International Drive (▷ 13) at night.

SWEET DREAMS

Hark back to days gone by at Disney's Grand Floridian (▷ 112) Victorian-style hotel.

Enjoy a touch of the Italian Riviera at Portofino Bay (▷ 112).

Drop anchor at the 1880s Nantucket-theme Disney's Yacht and Beach Club Resort (▷ 112) to get in touch with the ocean.

First-class service at Orlando's top hotels

HITTING THE SHOPS

Shop until you drop at the largest of them all—Orlando Premium Outlets (▷ 69).

Flex the credit card in the upscale stores at the Mall at Millenia (▷ 68).

Stock up on Americana and all things Native American in Old Town (▷ 34).

Don't forget your credit card on a visit to the shopping mall

TAKING IN A SHOW

Cheer for the knights of yore at Medieval Times (▷ 106).
Succumb to the romance and enchantment of Arabian Nights (▷ 36).
Marvel at the acrobatics and ballet at Cirque du Soleil®–La Nouba™ (▷ 37).

Go back in time to experience a joust and a fine dinner

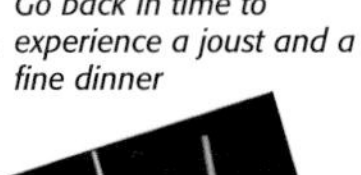

MOVIE MANIA

Dive into the undersea world of Princess Ariel during Voyage of the Little Mermaid (▷ 39).
Fight the off-world invaders with Men in Black™ Alien Attack™ (▷ 55).
Sing along to Hakuna Matata during Festival of the Lion King (▷ 38).

GETTING WET

Humunga Kowabunga is how you'll feel when you've tried this ride at Typhoon Lagoon (▷ 35).
Dodge water cannons on Popeye & Bluto's Bilge-Rat Barges® (▷ 50).
Get drenched by a whale at One Ocean—The Shamu® Show (▷ 64–65).
Take on The Storm at Wet 'n Wild (▷ 69).

Shamu at SeaWorld (above)

TEEING OFF

Play Greg Norman-designed courses and David Leadbetter Golf Academy at Championsgate (▷ 96).
Grande Lakes have also been designed by Greg Norman and feature Florida wetlands (▷ 97).
Disney's Palm course, designed by Joe Lee, can put you in hot water (▷ 39).

There are plenty of courses to practice your swing

Orlando by Area

© Disney

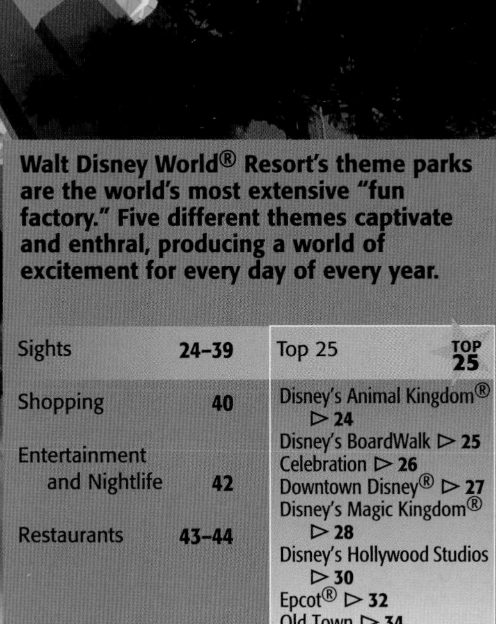

Walt Disney World® Resort's theme parks are the world's most extensive "fun factory." Five different themes captivate and enthral, producing a world of excitement for every day of every year.

Top 25

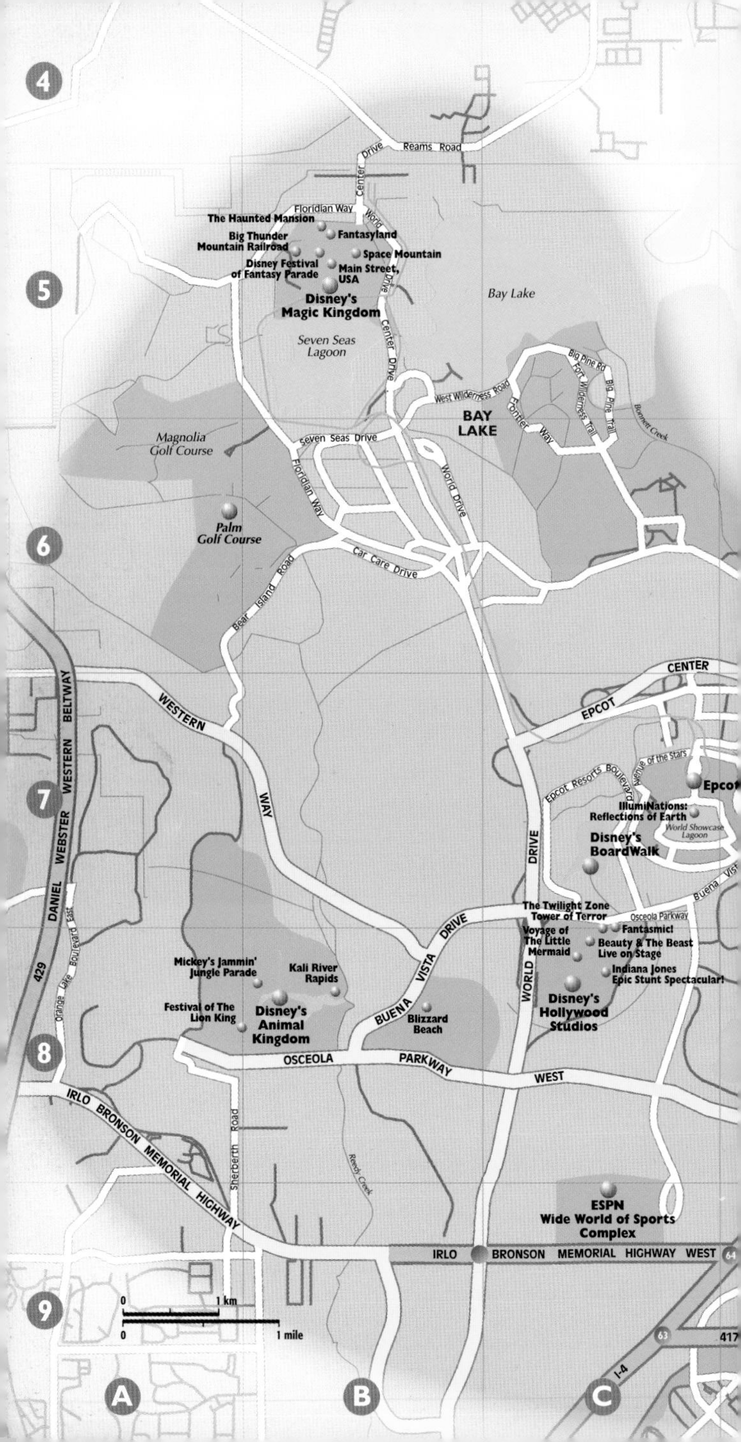

4
5
6
7
8
9
A
B
C
Reams Road
Center Drive
Floridian Way
World Drive
The Haunted Mansion
Fantasyland
Big Thunder Mountain Railroad
Space Mountain
Disney Festival of Fantasy Parade
Main Street, USA
Disney's Magic Kingdom
Bay Lake
Seven Seas Lagoon
Center Drive
Big Pine Rd
Fort Wilderness Trail
Big Pine Trail
West Wilderness Road
Frontier Way
BAY LAKE
Bonnett Creek
Seven Seas Drive
Magnolia Golf Course
Floridian Way
World Drive
Palm Golf Course
Car Care Drive
Bear Island Road
DANIEL WEBSTER WESTERN BELTWAY
WESTERN WAY
EPCOT CENTER
Avenue of the Stars
Epcot Resorts Boulevard
Epcot
IllumiNations: Reflections of Earth
World Showcase Lagoon
Disney's BoardWalk
WORLD DRIVE
Buena Vista
Osceola Parkway
The Twilight Zone Tower of Terror
Fantasmic!
Voyage of The Little Mermaid
Beauty & The Beast Live on Stage
Indiana Jones Epic Stunt Spectacular!
Disney's Hollywood Studios
BUENA VISTA DRIVE
Mickey's Jammin' Jungle Parade
Kali River Rapids
Festival of The Lion King
Disney's Animal Kingdom
Blizzard Beach
429
Orange Lake Boulevard East
OSCEOLA PARKWAY WEST
IRLO BRONSON MEMORIAL HIGHWAY
Sherberth Road
Reedy Creek
ESPN Wide World of Sports Complex
IRLO BRONSON MEMORIAL HIGHWAY WEST
64
63
417
I-4
0
1 km
0
1 mile

Disney and Maingate

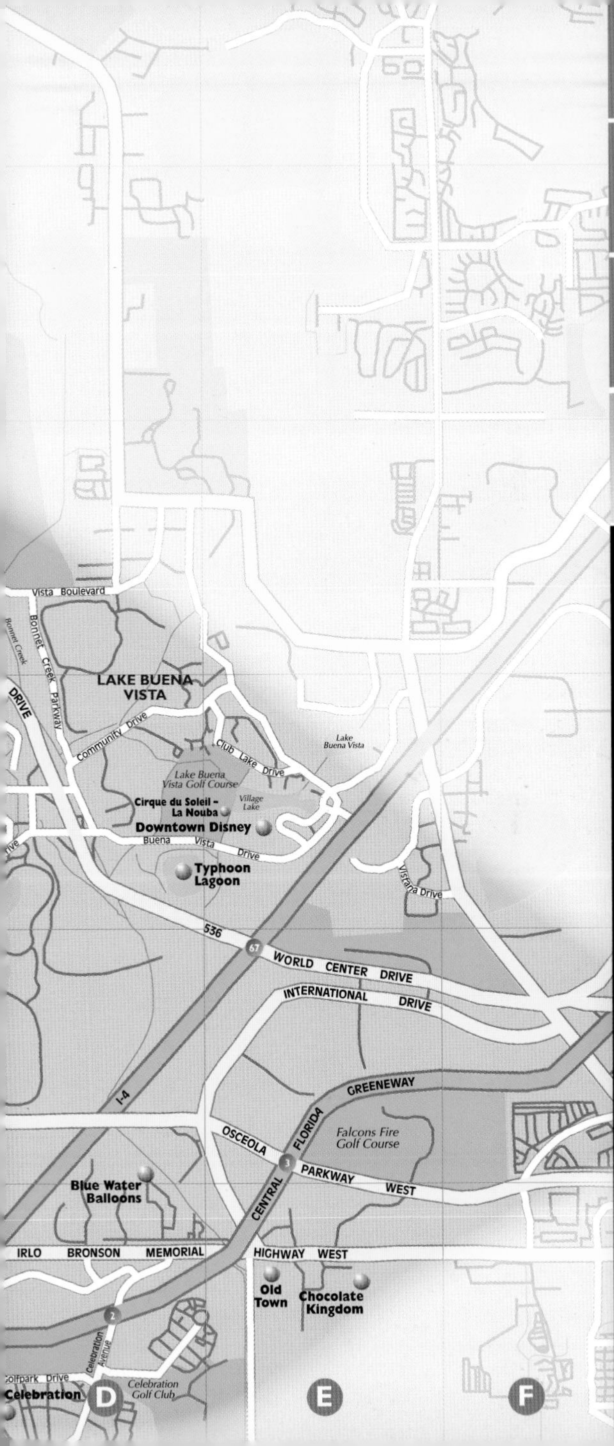

Vista Boulevard
Bonnet Creek
Bonnet Creek Parkway
DRIVE
LAKE BUENA VISTA
Community Drive
Club Lake Drive
Lake Buena Vista
Lake Buena Vista Golf Course
Village Lake
Cirque du Soleil – La Nouba
Downtown Disney
Buena Vista Drive
Typhoon Lagoon
Vistana Drive
536
67
WORLD CENTER DRIVE
INTERNATIONAL DRIVE
I-4
GREENEWAY
FLORIDA
OSCEOLA PARKWAY WEST
3
CENTRAL
Falcons Fire Golf Course
Blue Water Balloons
IRLO BRONSON MEMORIAL HIGHWAY WEST
Old Town
Chocolate Kingdom
2
Celebration Avenue
Golfpark Drive
Celebration
Celebration Golf Club
D
E
F

Disney's Animal Kingdom®

All aboard for Expedition Everest (left); a more sedate, animal safari (right)

© Disney

© Disney

THE BASICS

http://disneyworld.disney.go.com

B8

Osceloa Parkway

407/939-5277

Core hours 9–5; open later in summer and holidays

Range of restaurants and cafés

Lynx route 301

Excellent

Very expensive

HIGHLIGHTS

- DINOSAUR
- Festival of the Lion King show (▷ 38)
- Flights of Wonder
- It's Tough To Be a Bug!® movie
- Kilimanjaro Safaris®
- Kali River Rapids® (▷ 38)
- Maharajah Jungle Trek®
- Pangani Forest Exploration Trail®

Disney's film *The Lion King* sowed the seeds for this, the most recent addition to the Walt Disney World® Resort. Around the core of an excellent safari park, Disney has wrapped its inimitable razzmatazz of rides and shows.

Getting your bearings The park is divided into several areas, the major two being Asia and Africa, with their live animal attractions. Disney's Animal Kingdom® theme park radiates from a central point, the Oasis, where you will find the Tree of Life, a 200ft (61m) baobab. Watch the It's Tough To Be a Bug!® 3-D movie here or enjoy the cartoon characters in Finding Nemo—The Musical.

Live animals Take a jeep tour on the sun-bleached plains of "Africa" in Kilimanjaro Safaris®, to see giraffes, antelope, hippos, rhinos and ostriches. On foot you can enjoy a family of gorillas at Pangani Forest Exploration Trail®. On the neighboring "Asia" continent stroll among the ruins of a temple at Maharajah Jungle Trek® to spot playful gibbons and Komodo dragons. Asia's big cat, the tiger, has its own 5-acre (2ha) lair.

Artificial delights Disney works its magic here with rides and shows. Flights of Wonder offers an entertaining insight into bird behavior. The most exciting rides are Asia's Kali River Rapids® and DinoLand's DINOSAUR.

Avatar arrives In 2013, Disney released plans for a grand expansion based on the movie *Avatar*.

Disney's BoardWalk Villas, Crescent Lake

TOP 25 Disney's BoardWalk

© Disney

Disney's homage to the heyday of east-coast holidaying becomes reality in this hotel and entertainment complex set on the shores of Crescent Lake. Styled like an old-fashioned seaside town, it evokes memories of the 1920s.

Old-world style Renowned architect Robert A. M. Stern, who also designed the American Revolution Center at Valley Forge, wanted to create somewhere for Disney guests to unwind surrounded by the nostalgic "funshine" of days gone by. The BoardWalk has the feel of a small town with an appealing mélange of architectural styles—neo-Gothic cottages with lookout towers, shingle roofs, wooden balconies and porches cozy up to art deco dormer bungalows. At the BoardWalk Inn, the main hotel, the rooms have a wonderfully relaxed quality, like sleepovers at Grandma's house, with sumptuous brass beds, homey quilts and chintz drapes.

Perfect wind down The wide wooden deck around the lakeshore invites leisurely strolling or simple contemplation. It gives access to a range of quality emporia, eateries and entertainment, including Disney's own microbrewery, Big River Grille and Brewing Works, an ESPN® franchise sports bar with 100 TV screens and Jellyrolls sing-along piano bar. The nightspots here have a strict over-21s policy, giving it a much more adult atmosphere than Downtown Disney® as you move into the evening, perfect for those who prefer a less frenetic scene.

THE BASICS

http://disneyworld.disney.go.com

C7

Epcot Resorts Boulevard

407/939-5277

Shops 10–9. Restaurants and bars 11am–midnight. Clubs 9pm–2am

Range of cafés and restaurants

Lynx route 303

Excellent

Free to BoardWalk; attractions expensive

HIGHLIGHTS

- The 1920s and 1930s resort styling
- Dueling piano players at Jellyrolls
- 100 screens of sports at ESPN® Sports Central

Celebration

TOP 25

Let's celebrate on Celebration Avenue (left) by playing in the fountains (right)

THE BASICS

www.celebration.fl.us
D9
FL 34747
Welcome Center 407/566-1201
24 hours
Range of restaurants and cafés
Lynx route 56
Very good
Free; carriage rides expensive
Cultural and community events held throughout the year. Farmers' market on Sunday morning (Oct–May)

HIGHLIGHTS

- The slower tempo of the town
- The traditional architecture
- The Sunday farmers' market (Oct–May)
- Strolling around the lake
- Browsing in the stores
- Carriage rides

In the 1990s Disney picked up on a lost thread of Walt's dream and the Epcot® experiment got a new lease of life and extra realism, fusing traditional aesthetics and values with contemporary technology.

The foundations The plans called for a new type of old-fashioned "hometown," the kind of town that feeds the imagination of American idealists. Celebration would include a lake with nature walks and cycle paths and wooden benches. Downtown shops would be intimate boutiques with sidewalks for browsing and ice-cream parlors from which to watch the world go by. The houses would look traditionally southeastern, with clapboard siding, a swing on the porch and a spick-and-span yard. Colonial Revival, Victorian and Craftsman styles created architectural variety, but overall homogeneity would be preserved by prescribed colors and finishes.

The finished product Ground was broken on a patch of native Florida landscape just south-east of the Walt Disney World® Resort in 1996. Today 9,000 Celebration residents benefit from modern amenities such as a hospital, high school, university campus, golf course and a 6,000sq ft (557sq m) fitness center. The downtown core makes a relaxing place to spend a few hours. "Caribbeanesque" Market Street is a welcoming place to combine a spot of shopping with a lazy lunch. Rest awhile by the lake before taking a carriage ride—or rent a cute electric car—for a tour around the impressive surrounding suburbs.

La Nouba™ *by Cirque du Soleil® (left); Lego dinosaur icon (right)*

TOP 25 Downtown Disney®

© Disney

© Lego

Disney's main entertainment and shopping complex has something for every member of the family. Three distinct spheres make up the whole, each with its own character and purpose.

Marketplace The Marketplace is Disney's "shopping central" if you don't hit the parks themselves (you don't need a park ticket to shop here). It brings together 20 shops with "mouse-approved" merchandise, interspersed with eateries.

Pleasure Island A 6-acre (2.5ha) entertainment complex, Pleasure Island is set off the shore of Village Lake and is accessible by three bridges (allowing Disney to control entry). It aims to provide family entertainment throughout the day and late into the evening, with a selection of live music and performance arts venues. There's also a mix of eateries and shopping suitable for all the family.

West Side Disney has gone all out to ensure quality at this 70-acre (28ha) shopping and entertainment complex. It is home to the unique Cirque du Soleil®–La Nouba™ show, and the House of Blues® with excellent live music. Enjoy the innovative menu at Wolfgang Puck® Café or eat Cuban at Bongo's Cuban Café™.

Downtown Disney transformed Downtown Disney is currently evolving, with a grand expansion of its shopping and entertainment spaces and an enhanced layout, and along with it comes a new name—Disney Springs.

THE BASICS

- E7
- Lake Buena Vista Drive
- 407/396-5277
- Daily 10am–11pm (bars and clubs until 2am)
- Several restaurants and fast-food eateries
- Lynx routes 50, 300, 301, 302, 303, 304, 305 and 306
- Excellent
- Free; access to Pleasure Island moderate

HIGHLIGHTS

- Cirque du Soleil®–La Nouba™
- House of Blues®
- Wolfgang Puck® Café

Disney's Magic Kingdom®

© Disney

© Disney

© Disney

HIGHLIGHTS

- Cinderella Castle
- Main Street USA (▷ 39)
- Pirates of the Caribbean
- Splash Mountain®
- Big Thunder Mountain Railroad® (▷ 36)
- The Haunted Mansion® (▷ 38)
- Peter Pan's Flight®
- Mickey's PhilharMagic®
- Space Mountain® (▷ 39
- Disney Festival of Fantasy Parade
- Buzz Lightyear's Space Ranger Spin®

TIP

- The Magic Kingdom Harmony Barber Shop will add wash-out glitter, fluorescent or glow-in-the-dark color to your hair for fun.

The original Disney park kick-started Orlando's meteoric rise to worldwide fame. Magic Kingdom® still captures the fairy-tale world of the Disney movies: prepare to be charmed and beguiled.

Getting your bearings Main Street USA, Disney's take on old-town America, is as familiar to the world as Broadway or Oxford Street. It's the artery that leads to the heart of Magic Kingdom® and from here to fabulous "lands"—Adventureland, Frontierland®, Liberty Square, Fantasyland and Tomorrowland®—that radiate out to form the limbs of the park.

A character wonderland The iconic fairytale Cinderella Castle, at the entrance to Fantasyland, symbolizes Magic Kingdom®, creating a sense

Clockwise from far left: take a trip with The Magic Carpets of Aladdin ride at Magic Kingdom®; your dreams could come true at the Wishes nighttime spectacular; the ultimate fairy-tale dream—Cinderella Castle; take the kids to Stitch's Great Escape!

of wonder and awe. The "imagineers" have gone to enormous lengths to get every detail right; even the street lamps on Main Street USA cast shadows in the shape of Mickey Mouse ears when the sun shines.

Just for fun Magic Kingdom® is all about pure escapism; there's no educational motive. Each land has its collection of rides and shows, from roller coasters to 3-D animations. Many of them link directly to Disney films, so Dumbo, Peter Pan, Winnie the Pooh, Snow White and, more recently, Buzz Lightyear put in an appearance. The more challenging rides take you to places you wouldn't otherwise go: mountain summits, haunted houses or even into outer space. Mickey Mouse and pals make appearances throughout the park, for those very popular photo opportunities.

THE BASICS

http://disneyworld.disney.go.com
B5
Seven Seas Drive, off World Drive
407/939-5277
Core hours daily 9–7, later depending on season
Restaurants and cafés
Lynx routes 50, 56 and 302
Excellent
Very expensive
Special parades and events for major holidays

Disney's Hollywood Studios

© Disney

© Disney

© Disney

HIGHLIGHTS

- The Twilight Zone Tower of Terror™ (▷ 39)
- Rock 'n' Roller Coaster® Starring Aerosmith
- Star Tours®—The Adventure Continues
- Indiana Jones™ Epic Stunt Spectacular! (▷ 38)
- Beauty and the Beast—Live on Stage (▷ 36)
- Fantasmic! (▷ 37)
- Voyage of the Little Mermaid (▷ 39)
- Muppet*Vision 3D
- The American Idol® Experience
- Disney's Hollywood Studios Backlot Tours

TIP

- Have a plastic hook fob on your belt loop to attach your hat to when you get on rides.

Disney's homage to the glory days of Hollywood movies is an energetic romp through its cinematographic history, pausing for breath at hit movies. Also, take a tour of working Disney studios.

Here we go The scene is set as you enter via Hollywood Boulevard, rigged out in its 1930s heyday. In many ways The Great Movie Ride® encapsulates the park. This high-speed train takes a whistle-stop tour around classics, from *Casablanca* to *Aliens*, giving each an extra thrill with the enhanced special effects. This is the park with Disney's best state-of-the-art electronic wizardry. Most of the rides at Disney's Hollywood Studios are oriented more to adults and teenagers than young children. There isn't the invisible film of fairy dust that hangs in the air at Disney's

Clockwise from far left: thrills and daring escapades at Disney's Hollywood Studios; with your heart, or maybe your stomach, in your mouth take a ride on the exciting Rock 'n' Roller Coaster® Starring Aerosmith; guests ride a tram in Catastrophe Canyon on a Studio Backlot Tour

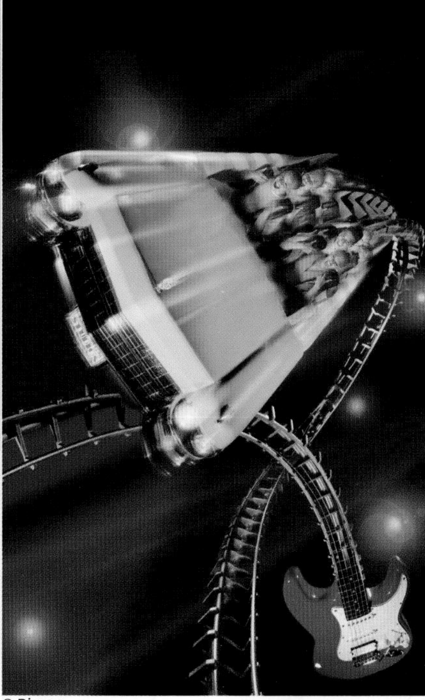

Magic Kingdom®, but the park makes up for that with several entertaining live shows, including film stunts explained in Indiana Jones™ Epic Stunt Spectacular! and the musical extravaganza Beauty and the Beast—Live on Stage.

Movie making About half the park is accessed by a guided backlot tour, offering a comprehensive view of whatever is being filmed at the time, whether it be a commercial or a full-length feature. Be aware, though, that much of the Disney cartoon production now takes place in California, so you'll have little chance of seeing Mickey come to life on celluloid. You'll be able to enjoy the special effects water tank, prop room and genuine backlots, climaxing in the Catastrophe Canyon ride where you find yourself taking part in the action.

THE BASICS

- C8
- North Studio Drive, off Buena Vista Drive
- 407/939-5277
- Core hours 9–7, extended hours depending on season
- Range of restaurants and cafés
- Lynx route 303
- Excellent
- Expensive
- Parades and celebrations throughout the year

Epcot®

TOP 25

© Disney

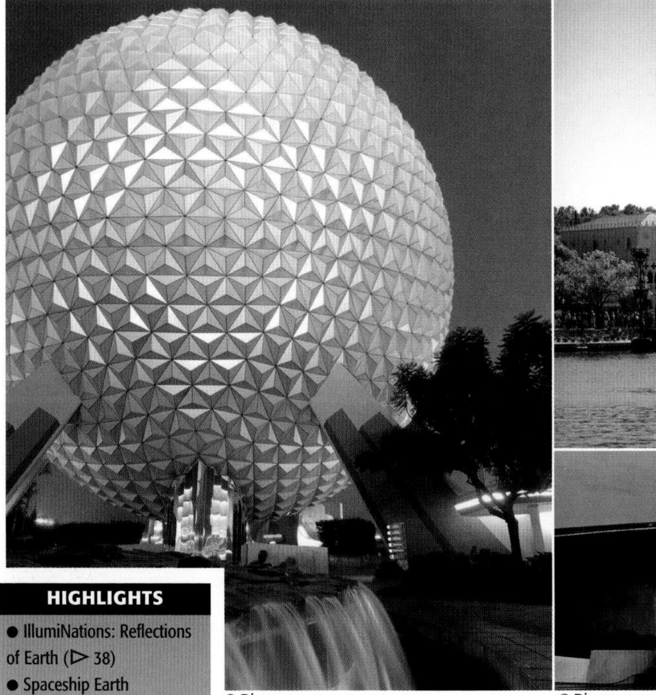

© Disney © Disney

HIGHLIGHTS

- IllumiNations: Reflections of Earth (▷ 38)
- Spaceship Earth
- The Seas with Nemo and Friends®
- Living with the Land
- Captain EO
- Test Track® Presented by Chevrolet®
- Mission: SPACE®
- Disney Phineas and Ferb: Agent P's World Showcase Adventure

TIP

- Club Cool is an ice tunnel with a drinks station offering free samples of sodas (pop) from around the world—a great place to cool down.

Epcot® was closest to Walt's heart. The experimental prototype Community of Tomorrow was to be a high-tech global village he hoped would act as a "think-tank" for the world's social problems.

Earth first Disney died before the concept was finalized and corporate Disney switched the emphasis from urban planning to Earth and technology. It delivers the fewest "thrills and spills" of Walt Disney World® Resort parks, but it's still lots of fun to explore.

Future perfect The emblem of Epcot®, the much-photographed golf-ball-like Spaceship Earth, sits at the heart of Future World. Play with the latest technological gadgets at the two Innoventions pavilions or dive deep into the physical world

Clockwise from far left: the icon of Epcot, the Spaceship Earth; take a whistle-stop tour around the world by visiting the pavilions of Italy (top middle) and Morocco (top right); the sun sets over the futuristic Spaceship Earth

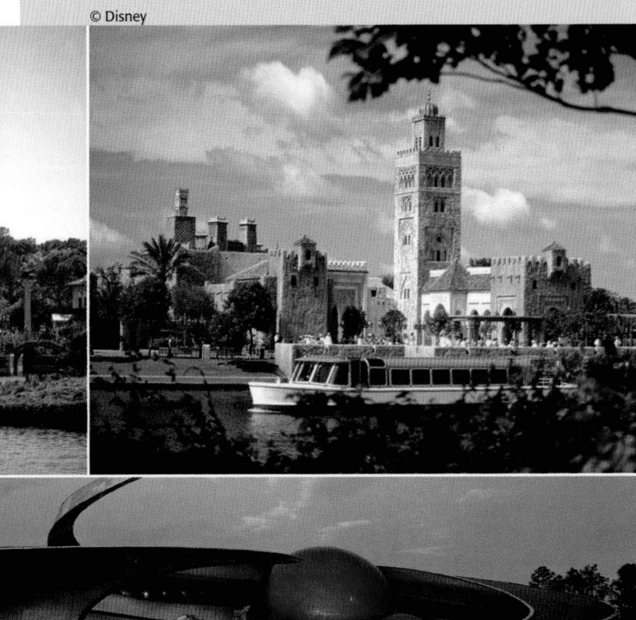

around you at The Seas with Nemo and Friends®, the Land or Ellen's Energy Adventure. If you can't spend a day in Orlando without doing a ride, go to Mission: SPACE®. This simulation puts you in one of NASA's missions, from the G-crunching launch to the weightlessness of orbit.

The world Set around an artificial lagoon, World Showcase has 11 geographical "zones" spanning four continents. Each featured country or continent presents itself in microcosm, offering the chance to explore its national specialties, architecture or consumer products, plus an assortment of artisans, minstrels, native flora and food. A whistle-stop tour around the world includes Morocco, Norway and Canada, but visit Japan with its Zen pagodas and rock gardens or France for the evocative film *Impressions de France*.

THE BASICS

http://disneyworld.disney.go.com
C7
Epcot Center Drive
407/939-5277
Future World daily 9–7. World Showcase daily 11–9
Range of restaurants and cafés
Lynx route 301
Excellent
Very expensive
Festivals throughout the year, International Food Festival in October

Old Town

TOP 25

Stroll down memory lane in Old Town, with its fine parade of classic US cars

THE BASICS

www.myoldtownusa.com
E9
5770 West US Highway 192
407/396-4888
Shops daily 10am–11pm. Amusements Mon–Fri 5–10pm, Sat–Sun 10am–11pm. Bars until 2am
Range of restaurants and cafés
Lynx routes 55 and 56
Very good
Free; rides inexpensive
Program of vehicular events throughout the year

HIGHLIGHTS

- Classic car parades
- Specialty shopping
- Old-fashioned fun fair
- Live music
- Hometown main street ambience

Head back to 1950s USA, where Rock 'n' Roll was a new craze and teenagers had just been invented. Frothy coffee was the drink of choice, blue jeans were tight and leather jackets obligatory.

Let's head into town Old Town is yet another Orlando "illusion." It re-creates that weekend across America when the fair rolled into town and everyone turned out to enjoy the fun. Bumper cars and a merry-go-round hark back to that era, while rides are brought up to date with the high-energy The Drop Zone and Super Shot, a kind of reverse bungee jump that offers a view of Kissimmee from 365ft (111m)—if you have the courage to open your eyes. In all there are 18 fairground rides catering from tots to adults. Along Old Town Main Street you'll find 75 specialty shops selling one-of-a-kind merchandise, from joke nametags and irreverent T-shirts to Native American crafts and healing crystals. There's live music every night on the Old Town stage.

Cruise Nite Old Town comes alive Thursday to Sunday with a chance for mods, rockers, Sharks and Jets to show off their "wheels." Saturday night is classic night with 300 pre-1970s automobiles, antiques and hot rods (parade starts at 8.30pm; cars assemble from 1pm). Friday night features cars from 1973 to 1987, including souped-up Corvettes and supercharged Mustangs (parade at 8.30pm, with cars assembling from 4pm). Thursday night is devoted to two wheels, as 700 leather-clad bikers show off their machines.

Ride the waves or swim in the depths—it's got it all at the lagoon

TOP 25

Typhoon Lagoon

© Disney

© Disney

Orlando's only disadvantage as a family holiday destination was its lack of beaches. So Disney stepped in to ensure that you won't miss sand between your toes or the sound of waves lapping onshore.

Why Typhoon Lagoon? Typhoon Lagoon is styled as a tropical harbor in the aftermath of a storm. Flotsam and jetsam, including a full-size shrimp boat beached on high ground, are strewn around. All water parks have the same basic ingredients, but two elements set 56-acre (22ha) Typhoon Lagoon apart from the others: the amazing surf pool and the amount of shade the park offers on a sunny day.

Action or relaxation? For adrenalin addicts, Humunga Kowabunga is the most thrilling ride. Riders hit 30mph (48kph) on this fully covered 2,100ft (640m) waterslide, and navigate a five-story drop before seeing the light of day. At the opposite end of the scale, spend a lazy 45 minutes exploring the misty rain forest, caves and grottos of Castaway Creek. Another impressive ride, Crush'n'Gusher, is high-speed fun.

Surf's up The Surf Pool offers something the Atlantic and Pacific can't match—a constant fetch consisting of perfect 5ft (1.5m) breakers every 90 seconds brimming with white foam. Forget about undercurrents or swells, and there are no rocks or sharks to spoil your day whether you ace or bail. For perfect technique, you can take surfing lessons (times vary by season, prebook).

THE BASICS

http://disneyworld.disney.go.com
D7
Off Buena Vista Drive
407/939-5277
Core hours 10–6, extended hours depending on season
Café
There are no direct bus services to the park
Excellent
Very expensive

HIGHLIGHTS

- Shark Reef
- Castaway Creek
- Humunga Kowabunga
- Surf Pool

More to See

BEAUTY AND THE BEAST—LIVE ON STAGE

Take a musical journey through this delightful Disney romance as Belle gradually falls in love with the Beast. The costumes and scenes are worthy of Broadway, as is the musical score.

✚ C8 ✉ Theater of the Stars, Disney's Hollywood Studios (▷ 30–31)

BIG THUNDER MOUNTAIN RAILROAD®

Oops! You're on a runaway steam train racing down a mountainside. Not the best coaster for thrills, but the animation and landscaping give it an edge.

✚ B5 ✉ Frontierland, Disney's Magic Kingdom® (▷ 28–29)

BLIZZARD BEACH

Disney's second water park is designed around a fake ski resort with several thrills. Summit Plummet is the world's tallest free-fall body slide.

✚ B8 ✉ Blizzard Beach Drive, off Buena Vista Drive, Lake Buena Vista ☎ 407/939-5277 🕒 Core hours 10–5, longer in summer 🍴 Cafés ♿ Excellent 💰 Expensive

BLUE WATER BALLOONS

www.bluewaterballoons.com

From 1,000ft (305m) up, you can get amazing views across Orlando and the theme parks, though the exact course depends on wind direction. Once this is achieved there's a champagne toast.

✚ D8 ✉ Box 560572, Orlando. Departure point Radisson Resort Orlando-Celebration ☎ 407/894-5040 or 407/749-0009 🕒 Daily, 1 hour before sunrise (weather permitting) 🍴 Breakfast included in ticket price ♿ None 💰 Very expensive

CHOCOLATE KINGDOM

www.chocolatekingdom.com

Want to know how chocolate is made or design your own chocolate bar? Then head to this walk-through exhibition and chocolate factory.

✚ E9 ✉ 2858 Florida Plaza Boulevard, Kissimmee ☎ 407/705-3475 🕒 Daily 11.30–7 (tours on the hour 12–6) ♿ Good 💰 Moderate

Racing through the canyon on the Big Thunder Mountain Railroad®

Plummeting down the slide at Blizzard Beach

CIRQUE DU SOLEIL®–LA NOUBA™

www.cirquedusoleil.com

Dance, mime, acrobatics and stunning visuals as the colorful cirque people clash with the dour urbanites for control of the earth.

E7 Downtown Disney, West Side (▷ 27) 407/939-7328 Tue–Sat at 6pm and 9pm Excellent Very expensive

DISNEY FESTIVAL OF FANTASY PARADE

Dancing along Main Street USA past Cinderella Castle, this mega-parade spins the best of Disney magic into one spectacle. A great mobile theater.

B5 Disney's Magic Kingdom® (▷ 28–29) Afternoon and early evening parade times vary, see park program

ESPN WIDE WORLD OF SPORTS® COMPLEX

State-of-the-art sports facilities that attract the Atlanta Braves football team for their spring training program (March), plus a host of other events.

C9 Victory Way, Lake Buena Vista 407/939-5277 Hours vary according to activity All Star café Excellent Expensive

FANTASMIC!

Mickey reprises his roll as the Sorcerer's Apprentice (from the Disney movie *Fantasia*), orchestrating a display of dancing fireworks, lasers and projected images to a wonderful musical score.

C8 Disney's Hollywood Studios (▷ 30–31) Evening when park is open late, see park program

FANTASYLAND

You'll find all Disney's characters here, so it's the perfect place for young children to meet Snow White, Dumbo or Peter Pan. The rides are generally gentle and make a great introduction to the roller coasters aimed at older kids.

B5 Disney's Magic Kingdom® (▷ 28–29)

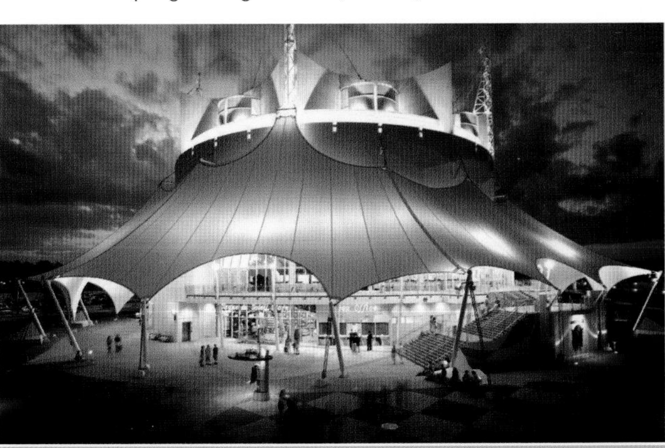

Roll up! Roll up! The Cirque du Soleil®–La Nouba™ is in town

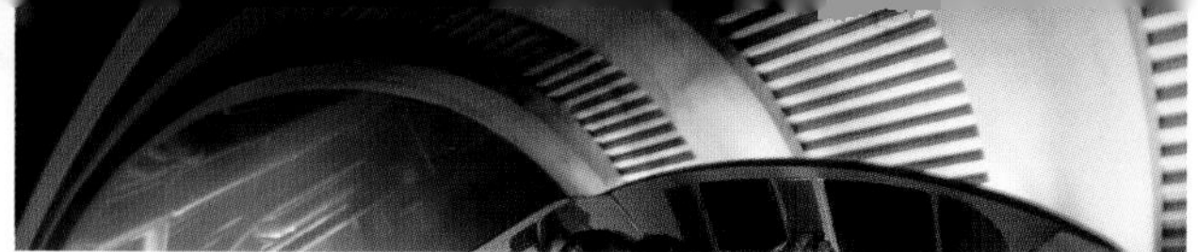

FESTIVAL OF THE LION KING

This show combines circus acts and parades, but it's the film's show tunes that really make the production; it soon becomes a great sing-along.

A8 Africa, Disney's Animal Kingdom® (▷ 24) Times vary, see park program

HAUNTED MANSION®

A motorized improvement of the old Haunted House fairground attraction, the fantastic special effects and gruesome antics will surprise and amaze those brave enough to enter here.

B5 Liberty Square, Disney's Magic Kingdom® (▷ 28–29)

ILLUMINATIONS: REFLECTIONS OF EARTH

This show is designed to encapsulate the life span of planet Earth, from the "Big Bang" to the present day. It can be difficult to follow the thread, so just enjoy it for the exceptional fireworks display that it is.

C7 World Showcase Lagoon, Epcot® (▷ 32–33) After dark but times vary so consult your park program

INDIANA JONES™ EPIC STUNT SPECTACULAR!

Want to know how those dangerous action sequences you see on adventure films are really done? Then this is the show for you.

C8 Disney's Hollywood Studios (▷ 30–31) Several shows per day. Times vary so consult your park program

KALI RIVER RAPIDS®

Take a white-water rafting trip down a tropical river. With water flowing freely over the rocks, every ride is different. One thing is certain, you'll get wet!

B8 Disney's Animal Kingdom® (▷ 24)

LAKE BUENA VISTA FACTORY STORES

www.lbvfs.com

This open-air mall wraps around its parking lot and has 125 outlet stores, including Gap, Old Navy and Nike. Try World of Coffee—great brew.

F8 15657 South Apopka-Vineland Road, Lake Buena Vista 407/238-9301 Mon–Sat 10–9.30, Sun 10–7 Cafés Lynx route 304 Very good Free

© Disney

Expect a drenching on the Kali River Rapids®

Main Street USA®

© Disney

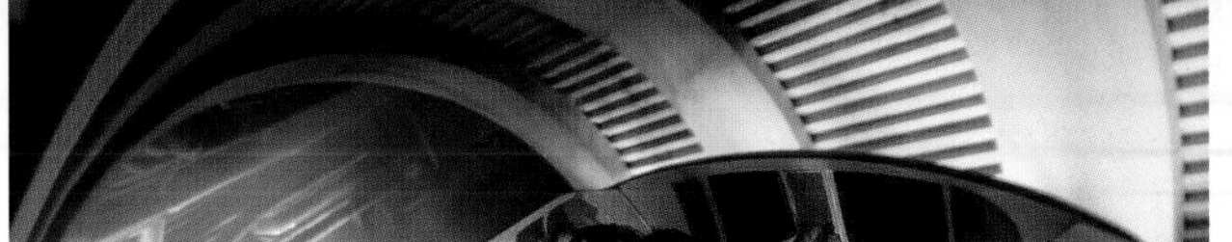

MAIN STREET, USA®

Surely one of the most photographed vistas in the world, the avenue that bisects Disney's Magic Kingdom leads the eye directly to Cinderella Castle. It couldn't be more picture perfect.

B5 Disney's Magic Kingdom® (▷ 28–29)

MICKEY'S JAMMIN' JUNGLE PARADE

Mickey and Minnie join Rafiki, Baloo and others for a party to celebrate the "animal kingdom."

B8 Disney's Animal Kingdom® (▷ 24) Afternoon, times vary so consult your park program

PALM GOLF COURSE

Designed by Joe Lee, it is renowned for its hazards, including several plays over water. Lessons and driving range also available.

A6 1950 West Magnolia/Palm Drive, Lake Buena Vista 407/939-5277; 407/939-4653 to book a tee time Tee times sunrise until 90 mins before sunset Café Excellent Very expensive

SPACE MOUNTAIN®

Take a ride through the solar system in this totally enclosed coaster. As your mind is fooled into thinking you are in outer space, the rails lead you into a series of switchback turns and short drops. The speed and visuals make it a great thrill.

B5 Tomorrowland, Disney's Magic Kingdom® (▷ 28–29)

THE TWILIGHT ZONE TOWER OF TERROR™

This Hollywood hotel is a high-tech development of the Haunted Mansion® (▷ opposite). Take the elevator and shortly after you enter the Twilight Zone™.

C8 Sunset Boulevard, Disney's Hollywood Studios (▷ 30–31)

VOYAGE OF THE LITTLE MERMAID

A romantic, musical journey, this is one of Disney's longest-running and best loved shows.

C8 Disney's Hollywood Studios (▷ 30–31) See park program

Perfect your drive on the Palm Golf Course

The chilling Twilight Zone Tower of Terror™. "The Twilight Zone" is a registered trademark of CBS, Inc. and is used pursuant to a license from CBS, Inc.

Shopping

ART OF DISNEY

A treasure-trove of all things Disney for the serious collector. Genuine Vinylmation and single cartoon cels make for unique souvenirs and gifts, plus there are limited edition figurines and paintings. This is very much a shop for older Disney fans and true aficionados.
B8 Future World, Epcot® 407/939-5277 Lynx route 301

THE BRASS BAZAAR

Authentic homeware from Morocco, including fantastic rustic pottery, turned brassware and inlaid wooden items.
C7 Morocco, World Showcase, Epcot® 407/939-5277 Lynx route 301

CUSTOM TAG SHOP

Have your own laser car registration tags printed with amusing messages or anecdotes. You can also buy laser key rings.
E9 Unit 303, Old Town, 5775 West US Highway 192, Kissimmee 407/397-4466 Lynx routes 55 and 56

DISNEY PIN TRADERS

Start a collection, trade for better or sell at this marketplace for Disney pin collectors.
E7 Downtown Disney Marketplace, Lake Buena Vista Drive, Lake Buena Vista 407/939-5277 Lynx routes 50, 300, 301, 302, 303, 304, 305 and 306

DISNEY'S WONDERFUL WORLD OF MEMORIES

"Scrap booking" is back in fashion and here you'll find lots of affordable ways to create a personal remembrance of your Disney visit.
E7 Downtown Disney Marketplace, Lake Buena Vista Drive, Lake Buena Vista 407/939-5277 Lynx routes 50, 300, 301, 302, 303, 304, 305 and 306

EMPORIUM

The Disney "one-stop shop" has a complete and comprehensive range of merchandise.
B5 Main Street USA®, Magic Kingdom® 407/939-5277 Lynx routes 56 and 302

LA NOUBA

Beguiled by the graceful aerial performances? Buy original artworks, themed items or DVDs to relive the show.
E7 Downtown Disney Marketplace, Lake Buena Vista Drive, Lake Buena Vista 407/ 939-5277 Lynx routes 50, 300, 301, 302, 303, 304, 305 and 306

THOSE HEAVY BAGS

All the major theme parks operate a system that allows you to forward any souvenir purchases to a central point to collect as you leave, so you don't need to carry them around all day with you.
If you are staying at a Walt Disney World® Resort hotel, any purchases made in any of their theme parks will be delivered to your hotel room while you continue to enjoy the rides and shows.

SOUVENIRS DE FRANCE

Lots of French-related items, from kitsch miniature Eiffel Towers to classic French produced arts and crafts, including hand-made soaps and printed Provençal fabrics.
C1 France, World Showcase, Epcot® 407/939-5277 Lynx route 301

STAGE 1 COMPANY STORE

A colorful emporium packed with your favorite Muppet souvenirs, plus memorabilia for fans of Phineas and Ferb. Miss Piggy and Kermit vie for space with Perry the Platypus on clothing, posters and pins.
C8 Streets of America, Disney's Hollywood Studios® 407/939-5277 Lynx route 303

WORLD OF DISNEY STORES®

The largest official Disney store outside the parks and reputedly the largest in the world. Whatever you're looking for, you should find it here.
E7 Downtown Disney Marketplace, Lake Buena Vista Drive, Lake Buena Vista 407/939-5277 Lynx routes 50, 300, 301, 302, 303, 304, 305 and 306

© Disney

Entertainment and Nightlife

AMC MOVIES AT DOWNTOWN DISNEY 24

Art deco-style movie complex showing the latest box office hits.
E7 Pleasure Island, Downtown Disney West Side, 1590 Buena Vista Drive, Lake Buena Vista 407/827-1308 Daily from 10am Lynx routes 50, 300, 301, 302, 303, 304, 305 and 306

ATLANTIC DANCE HALL

Disney's most up-to-date disco bar—with art deco styling—is where you can enjoy the current chart sounds. A vast screen shows non-stop videos. 21 minimum age limit.
C7 Disney BoardWalk, Epcot Resorts Boulevard 407/939-5277 Tue–Sat 9pm–2am Lynx route 303

BIG RIVER GRILLE AND BREWING WORKS

This microbrewery and eatery offers an inside view into how beer is made. Casual dining.
C7 Disney's BoardWalk, Epcot Resorts Boulevard 407/939-5277 Daily 11.30am–midnight Lynx route 303

DISNEY'S SPIRIT OF ALOHA SHOW

An open-air floorshow that features the music and dancing of the South Seas Islands, including a fire dance display. A buffet dinner is also served.
B6 Disney's Polynesian Resort, 1600 Seven Seas Drive, Lake Buena Vista 407/939-5277 Tue–Sat 5.15pm and 8pm Lynx route 302

HOOP-DEE-DO MUSICAL REVUE

A Wild West jamboree with banjo-toting cowboys at a campfire singsong.
C6 Pioneer Hall, Disney's Fort Wilderness Resort 407/939-3463 Seating at 5pm, 7.30pm and 9.30pm Lynx route 302

HOUSE OF BLUES®

www.houseofblues.com
Live acts, a great brunch and special guests make House of Blues a must for music lovers.
E7 Pleasure Island, Downtown Disney, 1490 Buena Vista Drive, Lake Buena Vista 407/934-BLUE (2583) Mon–Thu 8.30pm, Fri–Sun 9.30pm Lynx routes 50, 300, 301, 302, 303, 304, 305 and 306

WHAT'S ON

In the free newspaper *Orlando Weekly* you'll find comprehensive entertainment listings in categories from live music to sports events to exhibitions. The monthly *Orlando Magazine* offers articles about what's new and hot around the city so you can pick up on the city vibe, but its listings are limited to the major events and exhibitions.

JELLYROLLS

Named after "Jelly Roll" Morton, the resident pianists here take requests.
C7 Disney BoardWalk, Epcot Resorts Boulevard, Lake Buena Vista 407/939-5277 Daily 7pm–2am Lynx route 303

MARIACHI COBRE

This original Mexican band has played with singer Julio Iglesias. Their mariachi refrains fill the Mexico area of the World Showcase.
C7 Epcot, Box 10000, Lake Buena Vista 407/939-5277 Daily 11–9 Lynx route 301

RAGLAN ROAD™ IRISH PUB AND RESTAURANT

Traditional dancing, music and yarn-spinning from the Emerald Isle feature at this Irish pub.
E7 Pleasure Island, Downtown Disney, 1590 Buena Vista Drive, Lake Buena Vista 407/938-0300 Daily 11am–2am Lynx routes 50, 300, 301, 302, 303, 304, 305 and 306

SPLITSVILLE LUXURY LANES™

A great family entertainment complex based around a 30-lane bowling facility. There's live entertainment and an excellent casual eatery on site.
E7 Downtown Disney West Side 407/939-5277 Daily 10.30am–1am Lynx routes 50, 300, 301, 302, 303, 304, 305 and 306

PRICES

Prices are approximate, based on a 3-course meal for one person.

$$$ over $60
$$ $30–$60
$ under $30

1900 PARK FARE ($$)
Different characters join you at this breakfast or dinner buffet—check the noticeboards.
B5 Disney's Grand Floridian Resort, 4401 Grand Floridian Way, Lake Buena Vista 407/939-3463 Breakfast, dinner Lynx route 302

ARTIST POINT ($$)
Get a taste of America's northwest with Pacific salmon, buffalo and elk, plus regional wines.
B5 Disney's Wilderness Lodge 407/939-3463 Dinner Lynx route 302

BLUEZOO ($$$)
www.toddenglish.com
Todd English brings you exceptional seafood dishes from around the globe in this contemporary, neon-lit restaurant.
C7 Walt Disney World Dolphin Resort, 1500 Epcot Resorts Boulevard, Lake Buena Vista 407/934-1111 Dinner Lynx route 303

BONGO'S CUBAN CAFÉ™ ($$)
www.bongoscubancafe.com
Musicians Gloria and Emelio Estefan bring a taste of Cuba to Florida. The restaurant, in a pineapple-shaped building, evokes 1950s Cuba.
E7 Downtown Disney West Side 407/828-0999 Lunch, dinner Lynx routes 50, 300–306

CHEF MICKEY'S ($$)
Come here to dine with Mickey and friends.
B5 Disney's Contemporary Resort, 4600 North World Drive, Lake Buena Vista 407/939-3463 Breakfast 7am–11am, dinner 4pm–9.30pm Lynx route 302

CINDERELLA'S ROYAL TABLE ($$–$$$)
Enjoy a buffet breakfast with Disney characters.
B5 Cinderella Castle, Magic Kingdom 407/939-3463 Breakfast, lunch and dinner Lynx routes 50, 56 and 302

HAIL THE MOUSE

Despite several decades of Disney success, Mickey Mouse is the character every visitor wants to meet, whatever their age. Perhaps it is because the cheerful and ever optimistic rodent spans the age range, having debuted in an early talkie in 1928. Today Mickey is still going strong with his own TV show on the Disney Channel. He's omnipresent at Disney parks around the world. As Walt once said "...never lose sight of one fact... That this was all started by a mouse."

CITRICO'S ($$)
Northern Mediterranean dishes from France, Italy and Spain.
B5 Disney's Grand Floridian Resort, 4401 Grand Floridian Way, Lake Buena Vista 407/939-3463 Dinner Wed–Sun Lynx route 302

COLUMBIA RESTAURANT ($$)
One of Florida's oldest restaurants, Columbia serves tasty Spanish/Cuban food. Dine outside in a shady courtyard.
D9 649 Front Street, Celebration 407/566-1505 Lunch, dinner

CRYSTAL PALACE AT MAIN STREET ($$–$$$)
Pooh, Eeyore, Piglet and Tigger will join you for breakfast, lunch or dinner.
B5 Main Street, Magic Kingdom 407/939-3463 Breakfast, lunch, dinner Lynx routes 56 and 302

EARL OF SANDWICH ($)
This is the place to get rid of those hunger pangs, whatever time of day. Delicious freshly made sandwiches are the heart of the menu—try the signature roast beef—along with other casual eats, including soups and salads.
E7 Downtown Disney Marketplace 407/939-3463 Breakfast, lunch, dinner Lynx routes 50, 300, 301, 302, 303, 304, 305 and 306

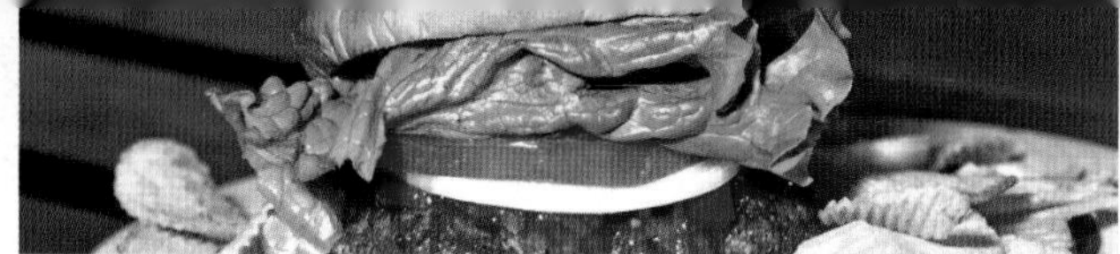

FULTON'S CRAB HOUSE ($–$$)
Step aboard this replica riverboat for some of the finest seafood around. If you prefer meat to fish, you can choose from a range of excellent aged steaks cooked to your exact requirements.
E7 Downtown Disney Pleasure Island 407/939-3463 Lunch, dinner Lynx routes 50, 300–306

GARDEN GRILL ($$)
A perfect place for a taste of Disney magic in the least "Disneyesque" park. The grill is graced with the presence of Mickey and Donald (dinner only).
C7 The Land, Futureworld, Epcot 407/939-3463 Lunch or dinner Lynx routes 301 and 303

KIMONOS ($$)
Graze on a few pieces of sushi for a quick bite or order a platter for a lavish dinner. Other Japanese dishes include Kobe beef and crispy tempura.
C7 Walt Disney World Swan Hotel 407/939-3463 Dinner Disney transport

KOUZZINA BY CAT CORA® ($$–$$$)
The mouthwatering Greek/Mediterranean menu is created by this popular celebrity chef. For breakfast try French toast baklava. At dinner, simple grilled fish, authentic pastitsio (Greek-style pasta), or slow cooked lamb shank all make delicious choices.
C7 Disney's Boardwalk 407/939-3463 Breakfast, dinner Lynx route 303

LIBERTY TREE TAVERN ($$)
The buffet is a year-round traditional Thanksgiving fare of roast turkey and other meats, with a selection of vegetables and sides.
B5 Magic Kingdom 407/939-3463 Dinner Lynx routes 56 and 302

PLANET HOLLYWOOD ($–$$)
Some of the best Hollywood and film memorabilia is on show here, with a full menu of standard burgers, grilled entrées and sandwiches.
E7 Downtown Disney, Buena Vista Drive, Lake Buena Vista 407/827-STAR (7827) Lunch, dinner Lynx routes 50, 300, 301, 302, 303, 304, 305 and 306

MEDITERRANEAN

Mediterranean cuisine is considered one of the healthiest in the world, resulting in a lower level of disease (certain cancers and heart disease) and a longer life span. What all these national cuisines have in common is a base of olive oil, delicious fresh salads and seasonal vegetables, a high proportion of seafood and an accompanying glass of red wine.

RAINFOREST CAFÉ® ($–$$)
The jungle canopies and animated wildlife of this café make it an exciting setting for a family meal of burgers, pizzas or steaks.
E7 Downtown Disney, East Lake Buena Vista Drive 407/827-8500 Lunch, dinner Lynx routes 50, 300–306

RESTAURANT MARRAKESH ($$–$$$)
Moroccan cuisine with great couscous and spit-roasted lamb.
C7 Morocco, World Showcase, Epcot 407/939-3463 Lunch, dinner Lynx routes 301 and 303

THE SCI-FI DINE-IN THEATER RESTAURANT ($)
Waitstaff on roller skates bring American fast food at this '50s-style diner. Burgers and hot dogs are the most popular choices.
C8 Disney's Hollywood Studios, Buena Vista Drive, Lake Buena Vista 407/939-3463 Lunch, dinner Lynx route 303

VICTORIA AND ALBERT'S ($$$)
The elegant surroundings and impeccable service are matched by a contemporary menu that changes daily. The fixed-price menus extend to 7 or 10 courses.
B5 Disney's Grand Floridian Resort & Spa 407/939-3463 Dinner Disney transport

Universal

Universal's two parks offer a world of comic characters and Hollywood-inspired rides, and coasters especially designed for adrenalin junkies. Linking the parks is CityWalk®, Universal's entertainment complex.

1
2
3
4
LAKE CANE HILLS
Lake Floy
Lake Cane
Turkey Lake Road
Vineland Road West
KIRKMAN ROAD SOUTH
Universal Studios
MEN IN BLACK Alien Attack
Beetlejuice's Graveyard Revue
Lake Marsha
Terminator 2: 3-D
Revenge of the Mummy
TRANSFORMERS: The Ride-3D
Universal Blvd
Shrek 4-D
Dragon Challenge
Seuss Landing
Universal CityWalk
Harry Potter and the Forbidden Journey
75
Jurassic Park River Adventure
The Incredible Hulk Coaster
Dr Doom's Fearfall
The Amazing Adventures of Spider-Man
Dudley Do-Right's Ripsaw Falls
Hollywood Way
74B
Universal Studios Islands of Adventure
TURKEY LAKE ROAD
I-4
Wallace Drive
0
1 km
0
1 mile
F
G

H
J

Universal Studios® TOP 25

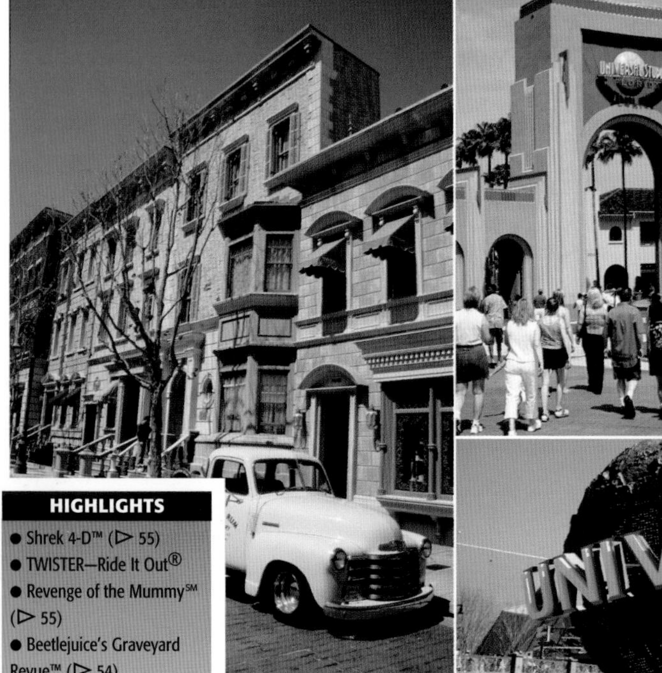

HIGHLIGHTS

- Shrek 4-D™ (▷ 55)
- TWISTER–Ride It Out®
- Revenge of the Mummy℠ (▷ 55)
- Beetlejuice's Graveyard Revue™ (▷ 54)
- Hollywood Rip Ride Rockit® (▷ 54)
- JAWS®
- MEN IN BLACK™ Alien Attack™ (▷ 55)
- The Simpson's Ride™
- Terminator 2®: 3-D (▷ 55)
- TRANSFORMERS: The Ride-3D

TIP

- Universal Express allows you to bypass the lines at all the rides at both parks (extra ticket cost except for guests at Universal Hotels).

Universal's arrival in Orlando gave adults something to cheer about. At last a park that didn't sugar coat the theme park experience and that didn't set an upper limit on exhilaration.

Basic principles Universal's vast catalog of box-office hits was fertile ground for ride "imagineers." The company developed the technological gadgetry that was revolutionizing Hollywood to use in a theme park: There's only one mainstream outdoor coaster ride here—Hollywood Rip Ride Rockit®. The buzz comes from robotics, pyrotechnics and 3-D visuals.

The experience The villains come in all shapes and sizes. Back from the future at Terminator 2®: 3-D, from outer space at MEN IN BLACK™

Clockwise from far left: a typical authentic studio set; outside Universal Studios; time for a break in a New York street scene at Universal Studios; classic cars outside the Hollywood Diner; the iconic Universal Globe welcomes visitors

Alien Attack™ and TRANSFORMERS: The Ride-3D and from the ancient past at Revenge of the Mummy℠. Nature plays its own powerful part at TWISTER-Ride It Out!® And JAWS®. Universal's cartoon stars allow younger visitors to get in on the act. Shrek and Donkey are on a quest to rescue Princess Fiona in Shrek 4-D™, while on The Simpson's Ride™ the Springfield family accompany you through Krustyville. The Wizarding World of Harry Potter® (▷ 51) expands into Universal Studios, where you'll find Diagon Alley™, linked to the Hogsmeade™ themed area in Universal's Islands of Adventure (you'll need tickets for both parks to cross areas).

Behind the scenes Universal is a working film studio and you can wander through the backlots to watch the latest scenes in progress.

THE BASICS

www.universalstudios.com
G2
1000 Universal Plaza
407/363-8000
Core hours Nov–Feb 9–6; Mar–Oct 9–7; extended hours by season
Range of restaurants and cafés
Lynx routes 21, 37 and 40
Excellent
Very expensive
Seasonal parties and parades on major holidays

Universal Studios Islands of Adventure®

HIGHLIGHTS

- Seuss Landing™ (▷ 55)
- Poseidon's Fury®
- Jurassic Park River Adventure® (▷ 55)
- Dudley Do-Right's Ripsaw Falls®
- The Amazing Adventures of Spider-Man® (▷ 54)
- The Incredible Hulk Coaster®
- Harry Potter and the Forbidden Journey™ (▷ 54)

TIP

- The Green Eggs and Ham Café™ at Seuss Landing™ really does serve green eggs.

Islands of Adventure®, Universal's second park, has true all-round appeal. Less adult-oriented than Univeral Studios®, it has excellent rides and attractions for all ages.

The idea For many of these rides Universal went back to basics. Sheer speed, stomach-turning drops and lots of water are the simple tools used to create sheer exhilaration, wrapped in convincing fantasy styling. The park consists of several "islands," most of which take a Universal or Nickelodeon theme.

Take the tour Marvel Super Hero Island® has two of the park's big-hitting attractions: the Amazing Adventures of Spider-Man®, with its astonishing special effects, and Incredible Hulk

Clockwise from top left: get a splashing with Popeye and Bluto's Bilge-Rat Barges; you'll need to get in line to visit the Lost Continent; welcome to the Islands of Adventure; the Islands of Adventure logo; you'll find plenty of theme shops in which to buy your superhero merchandise

Coaster®, which is a speed merchant's dream. You can immerse yourself in Popeye's watery world at Toon Lagoon. At the far reaches of the park, enter the primeval world of Jurassic Park, where designers have introduced the park's only "educational" element, the Discovery Center, filled with genuine bones and skeletons. Jurassic Park River Adventure® sends you hurtling through the ancient world, with a few surprises on the way. The marvelous magician and his friends invite you to Harry Potter and the Forbidden Journey™ at The Wizarding World of Harry Potter®, or take the high-speed Dragon Challenge® roller coaster. The Arabian Night's theme area the Lost Continent hosts The Eighth Voyage of Sinbad, the major show of islands of Adventure®. Last but not least is Seuss Landing™. For millions of *The Cat in the Hat* fans, it's a chance to meet their hero.

THE BASICS

www.universalorlando.com
G3
1000 Universal Plaza
407/363-8000
Core hours Nov–Feb 9–6; Mar–Oct 9–7; extended hours by season
Range of restaurants and cafés
Lynx routes 21, 37 and 40
Very good
Very expensive
Tours, lectures and special events

Take a drink at Pat O'Brien's, or a meal at Nascar—there's plenty to do on CityWalk

TOP 25 Universal CityWalk®

Dance the night away at the Shamrock 'n' Roll extravaganza on St. Patrick's Day, lubricated by green beer. CityWalk® doesn't need an excuse for a party, but if there is one, it pulls out all the stops.

The concept Universal trawled the playgrounds of North America and the Caribbean for inspiration for its self-contained entertainment complex, drawing on the most happening themes and venues. With its cafés, restaurants, eateries and clubs, it's an easy place to let the late afternoon post-park relaxation slip into an evening meal followed by a night on the town. It's all in one place.

The itinerary The evening always kicks off with live music or alive performance at CityWalk® Stage. You can stroll to the Big Easy, enjoy a Hurricane in Pat O'Brien's, then spend a few hours in Nassau savoring a margarita at Jimmy Buffet's® Margaritaville®, before "jetting" off to Jamaica for a rum at Bob Marley—A Tribute to Freedom™. Each venue brings a change of musical style including karaoke with a live band at CityWalk's Rising Star, and the all-inclusive ticket price means you don't need to pay at every door. If this itinerary sounds like a sure way to pick up a hangover, you're probably right, and it's wise to pace yourself. CityWalk® also allows you to combine activities for a set price. Take in an early movie at the multiplex cinema, then hit the clubs, or have a meal at one of the restaurants, then head to the dance floor. You can enjoy live concerts throughout the year on the open-air stage or at Hard Rock Live® auditorium.

THE BASICS

www.universalorlando.com

G2

1000 Universal Plaza

407/363-8000

Cafés open from 8am, restaurants from 11am, clubs from 4pm; ticket required for clubs after 8pm. Closes at 2am

Range of restaurants and cafés

Lynx routes 21, 37 and 40

Excellent

Access to CityWalk® is free, but there are admission fees (cheap) to clubs and the cinema complex. Hard Rock concerts very expensive

Seasonal parties and parades on major holidays and festivals

HIGHLIGHTS

- Bob Marley—A Tribute to Freedom™
- The Groove
- Hard Rock Cafe®
- Jimmy Buffet's® Margaritaville®
- Pat O'Brien's
- CityWalk's Rising Star
- Red Coconut Club℠

More to See

THE AMAZING ADVENTURES OF SPIDER-MAN®
Spider-Man hunts for thieves who have stolen the Statue of Liberty. The roller coaster is a combination of exceptional visual effects, track ride and live action, and a drop sequence.
G3 Marvel Super Hero Island®, Universal Studios Islands of Adventure® (▷ 50–51)

BEETLEJUICE'S GRAVEYARD REVUE™
Creepy Beetlejuice invites his ghoulish friends, Dracula, Frankenstein and his bride plus Wolfman, for a soft rock sing-along in this lively stage show.
G2 New York, Universal Studios® (▷ 48–49) 4 shows per day, times vary. See park program

DR. DOOM'S FEARFALL®
Rise 150ft (45m) into the air then drop like a stone faster than the force of gravity.
G3 Marvel Super Hero Island®, Universal Studios Islands of Adventure® (▷ 50–51)

HARRY POTTER AND THE FORBIDDEN JOURNEY™
Hogwarts™ is the setting for this incredible, ground-breaking adventure ride as you fly with Harry Potter and his companions in search of magical experiences.
G3 The Wizarding World of Harry Potter®, Universal Studios Islands of Adventure® (▷ 50–51)

HOLLYWOOD RIP RIDE ROCKIT®
Orlando's highest roller coaster reaches 17 stories (65ft/20m) above Universal. Choose a rock track to accompany your adventure, which becomes the backing track of the souvenir video of your ride (extra charge), then charge along at speeds of up to 65mph (105kph).
G2 Production Central, Universal Studios® (▷ 48–49)

INCREDIBLE HULK COASTER®
Twists, loops and drops are the order of the day. From the initial blast out of the start gate, it's thrilling to the final second.

A chilling experience at Beetlejuice's Graveyard Revue™

Hollywood Rip Ride Rockit®

G3 Marvel Super Hero Island®, Universal Studios Islands of Adventure® (▷ 50–51)

JURASSIC PARK RIVER ADVENTURE®

A cruise through tranquil Jurassic countryside goes wrong, ending in the longest, fastest and deepest drop of any water ride in Orlando.

G2 Jurassic Park, Universal Studios Islands of Adventure® (▷ 50–51)

MEN IN BLACK™ ALIEN ATTACK™

As an MiB agent, your first mission is to save the universe. Throughout the ride you try to amass points by killing the aliens, which adds to the fun.

G2 Universal Studios® (▷ 48–49)

REVENGE OF THE MUMMY®

Based on the *Mummy* action films, the special effects are on the same scale as the movie. A coaster propels you bullet-like into the thrills and scares of the 3-D special effects. Not for the fainthearted.

G2 New York, Universal Studios® (▷ 48–49)

SEUSS LANDING™

Immerse your children in the pastel-color world of Dr. Seuss. All their favorite characters are here, including Thing One and Thing Two.

G3 Universal Studios Islands of Adventure® (▷ 50–51)

SHREK 4-D™

Lord Farquaad comes back from the dead in an attempt to reclaim his bride, Princess Fiona, from *Shrek* in this entertaining 4-D film show.

G2 Production Central, Universal Studios® (▷ 48–49) Shows throughout the day

TERMINATOR 2®: 3-D

Not so much a ride as an experience; you'll be in the middle of the action as Cyberdyne Systems seems set to take over the world before the Terminator makes his appearance.

G2 Hollywood, Universal Studios® (▷ 48–49)

Shrek to the rescue

Prepare to be scared on the Jurassic Park River Adventure®

Shopping

ALL THE BOOKS YOU CAN READ
All of Dr. Seuss's rhyming stories can be found here in print or CD/DVD, so you can revisit these zany couplets or introduce them to the kids.
G3 Seuss Landing, Islands of Adventure
407/224-5800 Lynx routes 21, 37 and 40

COMIC BOOK SHOP
Sells a wide range of comics and collections for all your most popular characters.
G3 Marvel Super Hero Island, Islands of Adventure 407/224-5800
Lynx routes 21, 37 and 40

DERVISH AND BANGES®
All wannabee Hogwarts' pupils should stop off here for their school supplies, including replica uniforms, The Monster Book of Monsters, and Quidditch™ equipment. For "casual Fridays" there's a range of Potteresque T-shirts and informal apparel.
G3 The Wizarding World of Harry Potter, Universal Studios Islands of Adventure 407/224-5800
Lynx routes 21, 37 and 40

DINOSTORE℠
There's a whole range of "dino"-related merchandise here, from the serious scientific and educational material for would-be archeologists to fun stuff.
G3 Jurassic Park, Islands of Adventure
407/224-5800 Lynx routes 21, 37 and 40

ENDANGERED SPECIES STORE®
Merchandise related to endangered animals and ecosystems. Items include cute and cuddly toys and educational games and books.
G2 CityWalk
407/224-5800 Lynx routes 21, 37 and 40

THE MARVEL ALTERNIVERSE STORE®
Merchandise for all your favorite Marvel comic characters can be found here, all under one roof.

A MARVELOUS HISTORY
Marvel heroes arrived in the 1940s when Human Torch and Submariner fought the Nazis. In the 1950s, the publishers fell foul of the McCarthy Trials, but during the early 1960s, the Fantastic Four, the Incredible Hulk and Spider-Man were launched. By the late 1960s Marvel Comics cartoons hit TV screens. In the 1970s, the X-Men, Conan the Barbarian and Red Sonja were introduced and the Incredible Hulk debuted on TV. Marvel was elevated to the big screen with *X-Men* (2000), *Spider-Man* (2002), *Fantastic Four* (2005) and *The Incredible Hulk* and *Iron Man* (2008).

G3 Marvel Super Hero Island, Islands of Adventure 407/224-5800
Lynx routes 21, 37 and 40

MIB GEAR
Buy Men in Black-theme souvenirs, including the signature black sunglasses and replica ray guns.
G2 World Expo, Universal Studios
407/224-5800 Lynx routes 21, 37 and 40

SUPPLY VAULT
Stock up on Transformer's merchandise, including N.E.S.T. combat gear, bags, jewelry, mugs, key fobs and, of course, lots of action figures.
G2 Production Central, Universal Studios
407/224-5800 Lynx routes 21, 37 and 40

UNIVERSAL STUDIOS STORE®
A great place to shop if you don't want to enter the Universal parks. A good range of Universal and Islands of Adventure merchandise.
G2 CityWalk, Universal Boulevard
407/363-8000 Lynx routes 21, 37 and 40

UNIVERSAL STUDIOS STORE®
A comprehensive range of Universal souvenirs on the main thoroughfare close to the entrance/exit.
G2 Plaza of the Stars, Universal Studios
407/224-5800 Lynx routes 22, 37 and 40

Entertainment and Nightlife

BLUE MAN GROUP

This trio has a unique take on the world, combining pop music with pop art in a visually stunning show now in residence at Universal Studios®.

G2 Blue Man Group Theater, CityWalk 407/224-5800 or 888/340-5476 Check for times Lynx routes 21, 37 and 40

BOB MARLEY—A TRIBUTE TO FREEDOM™

Listen to live reggae music nightly in the open-air gazebo.

G2 CityWalk, 1000 Universal Studios Plaza 407/224-3663 Daily 4pm–2am Lynx routes 21, 37 and 40

CITYWALK'S RISING STAR

Universal's karaoke bar has one major difference over the competition, you'll have a live band with you on stage, not a recording sound box. It can't get more real than this—imagine yourself on *X-Factor* or *American Idol* and give it your best shot!

G2 CityWalk 407/224-5800 Daily 4pm–2am Lynx routes 21, 37 and 40

THE GROOVE

The best in dance music from the '70s to today, The Groove caters to age groups 20s to 50s.

G2 CityWalk, Universal Boulevard Plaza 407/224-8000 Daily 9pm–2am Lynx routes 21, 37 and 40

HARD ROCK LIVE

A regular program of artists appear live at the 3,000-seater Hard Rock Stadium, and the music covers all genres. Recent artists who have trodden the boards have included Willie Nelson, Snow Patrol and Meatloaf. Tickets sell out very quickly so check well in advance.

G2 CityWalk 407/351-5483 Check for times of individual performances Lynx routes 21, 37 and 40

JIMMY BUFFET'S® MARGARITAVILLE®

This is a little corner of the Bahamas in Orlando. Soak up the sunshine and a cocktail on one of the balconies or on the patio. Jimmy Buffet's tunes offer a lilting soundtrack.

G2 CityWalk, 6000 Universal Boulevard 407/224-2155 Nightly 11am–2am Lynx routes 21, 37 and 40

COCKTAILS

Cocktails are an integral part of the party scene in Orlando, so you'll need to get the lowdown on what to order.

Daiquiri—Jamaica rum, lime and powdered sugar

Margarita—tequila, triple sec and a dash of lime juice

Martini—vodka or gin with a dash of vermouth

Pina Colada—light rum, pineapple juice and coconut cream

Tequila Sunrise—tequila, orange juice and cranberry juice

PAT O'BRIEN'S

Pat O'Brien opened his bar in Bourbon Street, New Orleans in 1933. His "Hurricane" cocktail soon made it famous. Pat O'Brien's at CityWalk brings the Big Easy to Orlando. It's Mardi Gras all year here.

G2 CityWalk 407/224-5800 Nightly 4pm–2am Lynx routes 21, 37 and 40

RED COCONUT CLUB®

Universal's take on the "lounge" culture that is so fashionable nowadays, the Red Coconut turns seamlessly from drinks venue into nightclub. Try the signature martinis.

G2 CityWalk 407/224-2425 Sun–Wed 7pm–2am, Thu–Sat 6pm–2am Lynx routes 21, 37 and 40

UNIVERSAL CINEPLEX

The only multicinema complex to offer beer and wine to enhance your viewing pleasure. Multiscreens offer the latest movies.

G2 CityWalk 407/354-5998 Showings 12–11pm Lynx routes 21, 37 and 40

Restaurants

PRICES

Prices are approximate, based on a 3-course meal for one person.
$$$ over $60
$$ $30–$60
$ under $30

EMERIL'S ($$$)

Chef Emeril Lagasse resurrected the Cajun/ Creole cuisine of New Orleans. Start with a New Orleans cocktail then try his sauces on chicken, meat and andouille sausage.
G2 CityWalk, 6000 Universal Boulevard, 407/224-2424 Lunch, dinner Lynx routes 21, 37 and 40

EMERIL'S TCHOUP CHOP ($$$)

Pronounced chop-chop, Emeril's latest Orlando venture melds Pacific and Oriental flavors to produce delicious stir-fries and salads, along with inventive entrées. Emeril's signature dishes never fail to deliver.
G3 Royal Pacific Resort, Universal Studios, 6300 Hollywood Way 407/503-2467 Lunch, dinner

HARD ROCK CAFE ($$)

The largest in this chain of cafés, Hard Rock Orlando also has its most in-depth collection of rock memorabilia.
G2 CityWalk 407/351-7625 Lunch, dinner Lynx routes 21, 37 and 40

JIMMY BUFFET'S® MARGARITAVILLE® ($$)

Crooner Jimmy Buffet offers his take on the Caribbean with cocktails and simple yet delicious food. Buffet's music plays during the day and he sometimes puts in a live appearance.
G2 CityWalk, 6000 Universal Boulevard 407/224-2155 Lunch, dinner Lynx routes 21, 37 and 40

LOMBARD'S SEAFOOD GRILLE ($$)

Full-service restaurant overlooking the lake in the park, Lombard's serves excellent fresh seafood, superb chowder and a range of pastas and salads.
G2 Amnity, Universal Studios 407/224-3613 Lunch, dinner Lynx routes 21, 37 and 40

EMERIL FACTS

Things you may not know about chef Emeril Lagasse:

- He spent his childhood in Fall River, Massachusetts
- After graduation he was offered a music scholarship
- He opened his first restaurant, Emeril's in New Orleans, in 1990. He now has 14
- His 19 cookbooks have sold over 4 million copies
- He has hosted over 2,000 shows on American TV
- In 2013 he was awarded the Humanitarian of the Year award by the James Beard Foundation
- He raised $5.5 million for charity

MEL'S DRIVE IN ($–$$)

Themed on the diner in the movie *American Graffiti,* Mel's serves authentic burgers, hot dogs and milk shakes.
G2 Universal Studios 407/363-8000 During park hours Lynx routes 21, 37 and 40

MYTHOS RESTAURANT ($–$$)

A full-service restaurant with contemporary cuisine complemented by fast food staples.
G2 Islands of Adventure 407/224-5800 Lunch Lynx routes 21, 37 and 40

NASCAR® SPORTS GRILLE ($–$$)

This official NASCAR restaurant has great cars outside and table-side plasma screens. Signature ribs, burgers and sand-wiches are on the menu.
G2 CityWalk 407/224-RACE (7223) Lunch, dinner Lynx routes 21, 37 and 40

PALM ($$–$$$)

Enjoy excellent steaks and chops, and the cartoons on the walls of this offshoot of the New York Palms.
G2 Hard Rock Hotel, Universal Studios 407/503-7256 Dinner

Orlando's first tourist district still pulls in the crowds with a vast selection of hotels, restaurants and independent attractions. It's also a mecca for shoppers and includes two outstanding outlet centers.

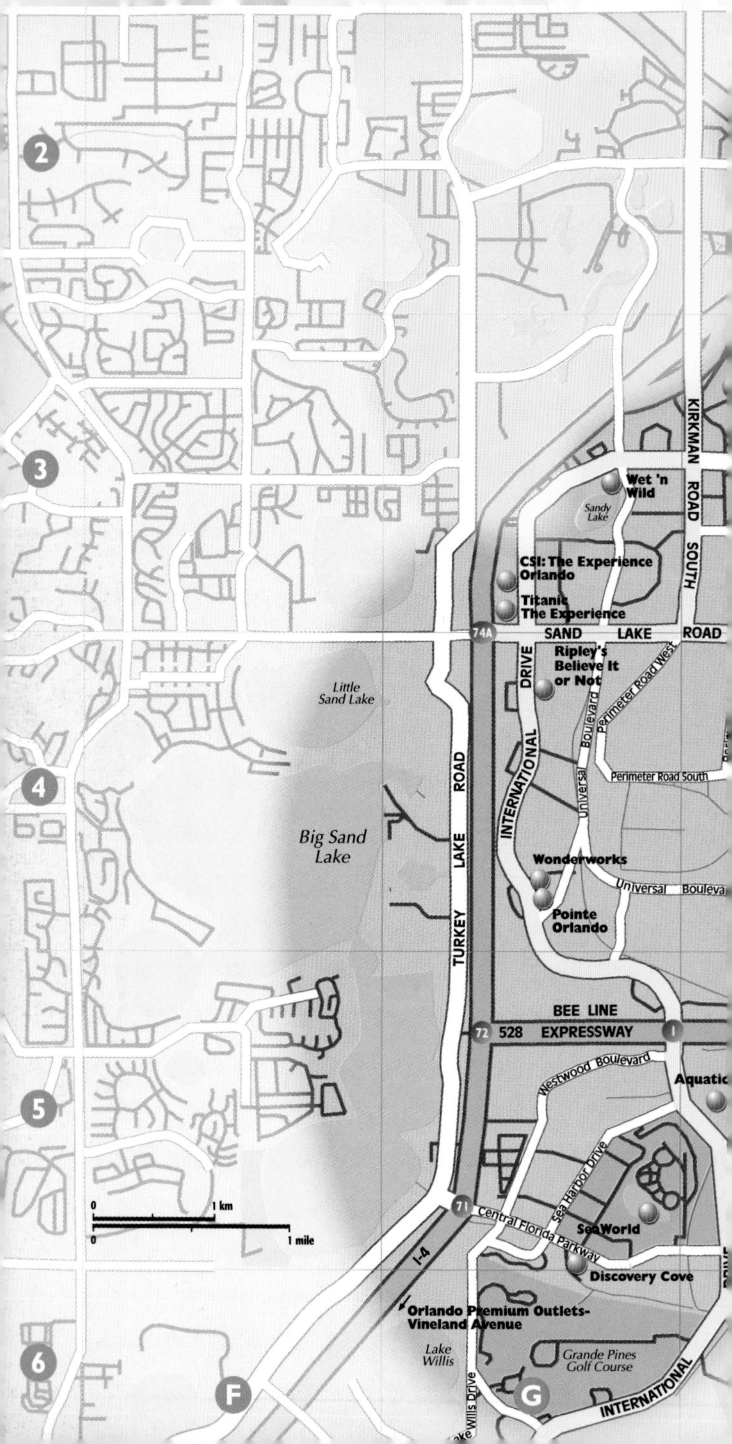
2
3
4
5
6
F
G
KIRKMAN ROAD SOUTH
Wet 'n Wild
Sandy Lake
CSI: The Experience Orlando
Titanic The Experience
74A
SAND LAKE ROAD
Ripley's Believe It or Not
INTERNATIONAL DRIVE
Universal Boulevard
Perimeter Road West
Perimeter Road South
Little Sand Lake
Big Sand Lake
TURKEY LAKE ROAD
Wonderworks
Universal Boulevard
Pointe Orlando
BEE LINE
72
528 EXPRESSWAY
1
Westwood Boulevard
Aquatic
Sea Harbor Drive
71
Central Florida Parkway
SeaWorld
Discovery Cove
0
1 km
0
1 mile
I-4
Orlando Premium Outlets-Vineland Avenue
Lake Willis
Lake Willis Drive
Grande Pines Golf Course
INTERNATIONAL

The Holy Land Experience
78
Americana
Boulevard
Road
Vineland
Road
Tropical Lake
The Mall at Millenia
77
259
Radebaugh
Ligustrum Way
Brookgreen Avenue
Seabridge Drive
Orlando Premium Outlets-International Drive
OAK
RIDGE
ROAD
WEST
FLORIDA'S
TURNPIKE
Drive
Elderberry
un Spot America
rlando
ebounderz
Vanguard
Street
Mandarin Drive
TANGELO PARK
Anzio
Street
Municipal Drive
Nectar Drive
Steyer
St
WEST
H
J

Discovery Cove

TOP 25

Interacting with dolphins is the order of the day at Discovery Cove

THE BASICS

www.discoverycove.com
G5
6000 Discovery Cove Way
877/577-7404
Daily 8–5.30 (check-in starts at 7.30)
Restaurant and café (included in the ticket price)
Lynx routes 8, 38 and 50; I-Ride
Excellent
Very expensive (all inclusive of meals, snacks, equipment and pass to SeaWorld)

HIGHLIGHTS

- Lagoon
- Coral Reef
- Ray Lagoon
- Tropical River
- Aviary
- Beaches

One of Orlando's major attractions, and sibling of SeaWorld, Discovery Cove was opened in 2000 after research showed that visitors were looking for a more intimate, personal vacation experience.

The perfect hideaway The park is designed around a tropical lagoon with white-sand beaches, swaying palms and hammocks. It feels like a tropical resort with no crowds, no lines—just a chance to chill out.

Let's make a new friend Discovery Cove's highlight is the Dolphin Encounter, a personal interaction with one of nature's most lovable creatures. Small groups of eight or so people, guided by a trainer, head into the dolphin pool for a well-orchestrated interaction.

Exploring Discovery Cove While you wait for your encounter—the undoubted highlight of your day—you can enjoy the other environments around the park. Swim and snorkel among shoals of tropical fish at the Coral Reef or get up close and personal with rays at Ray Lagoon. The Tropical River offers the chance to drift along in warmer waters and relax beneath the cascades, while the Aviary has over 250 exotic birds, many of which will feed from your hand.

Trainer for a day This package lets you spend extra time behind the scenes learning what it's like to look after dolphins. There's time in the water with them and a private photo session.

Shopping is just one of several attractions at Pointe Orlando

TOP 25

Pointe Orlando

Sitting at a busy intersection, on a prime spot surrounded by hotels and within walking distance of Orange County Convention Center, Pointe Orlando is International Drive's primary entertainment hub.

Let's get to the Pointe Though Pointe Orlando is smaller than Downtown Disney or CityWalk, it draws people with its good range of eateries, shops and nightlife attractions.

Hungry? There are restaurants aplenty, from family-friendly to elegant spots for couples. Enjoy the all-day diner-style menu at Johnny Rocket's, or excellent steaks at The Capital Grille. Try the Mediterranean medley at Maggiano's Little Italy and Greek Taverna Opa or the Caribbean choices at Cuba Libre Restaurant and Rum Bar.

Entertainment for the whole family Monkey Joe's play center is designed for younger kids (2–11), and the 20-theater Regal cinema caters to everyone. Wonderworks (▷ 66) is an exciting hands-on exploration of science for kids of all ages. Adult fun starts later in the evening (after 9pm), at the acclaimed B.B. King's Blues Club or the Improv Comedy Club. Both venues also offer full service menus.

Browsing and buying Pointe Orlando has a small selection of main-street names and some interesting stores not found in the other malls. These include Chico's ladies wear, Image Leather and Tharoo & Co jewelers.

THE BASICS

www.pointeorlando.com
G4
9101 International Drive
407/248-2838
Oct–May Mon–Sat 12–10, Sun 12–8; Jun–Sep Fri–Sat 12–9, Sun–Thu 12–8. Bars and restaurants may open later
Cafés and restaurants
Lynx routes 8, 38, 42, 58 and 111; I-Ride
Excellent

HIGHLIGHTS

- B.B. King's Blues Club (▷ 72)
- Improv Comedy Club (▷ 72)
- Wonderworks (▷ 66)

TIP

- At busy convention times many restaurants get booked out for private functions, so ring ahead for availability.

SeaWorld

TOP 25

HIGHLIGHTS

- One Ocean—The Shamu® Show
- Dolphin Cove
- Antarctica Empire of the Penguin
- Wild Arctic
- Kraken
- Shark Encounter
- Clyde and Seamore Take Pirate Island

TIP

- Between October and April bring a change of clothes if you sit at the front for The Shamu® Show because you may get wet and feel cold.

Bringing the ocean's life to Orlando, SeaWorld is a combination of aquatic zoo, animal encounters and shows. It's also a research and rescue facility for rare or sick marine creatures.

Let's explore The park is divided into a number of different sectors with water temperatures from freezing to tropical to accommodate their inhabitants. Dolphin Cove is one of the most popular areas. The dolphins playfully skirt the edges of the environment so that everyone gets a chance to stroke their flanks. Close by, there's a dolphin nursery where you can catch up with the latest arrivals. Manatees are one of the most endangered of Florida's native creatures and these huge salad eaters—also known as sea cows—have their own quiet corner to live in. The manatee

Clockwise from far left: on the way to the ultimate ocean experience at SeaWorld; take the Journey to Atlantis Ride; look behind you—one of the marine residents of SeaWorld; Turtle Trek; the Manta® roller coaster; SeaWorld sign; what's up?—sea lion at the Pirate Island Show

rescue program has so far saved more than 270 animals. In contrast to the warm tropical waters of the manatee enclosure are two major attractions that bring the icy cold to Florida. Wild Arctic is an excellent, though frosty, encounter with polar bears, one of the far north's most awe-inspiring mammals, while Antarctica Empire of the Penguin, Seaworld's newest attraction, features a state-of-the-art ride through a penguin's world.

Other attractions Shamu the Killer Whale is the emblem of the park and he's the leading star in his own show called One Ocean. Other equally entertaining shows include Clyde and Seamore Take Pirate Island, starring a hilarious sea lion and otter double act. SeaWorld has also bowed to pressure and built two rides, the watery Journey to Atlantis and Kraken, an amazing roller coaster.

THE BASICS

www.seaworld.com
G5
7007 SeaWorld Drive
888/800-5447
Core hours Mar–Oct 9–7 (later in summer); Nov–Feb 9–6
Restaurants and several cafés
Lynx routes 8, 38, 50 and 111; I-Ride
Excellent
Very expensive
Seasonal special events

Wonderworks

TOP 25

There's a whole world of experiences and experiments at topsy-turvy Wonderworks

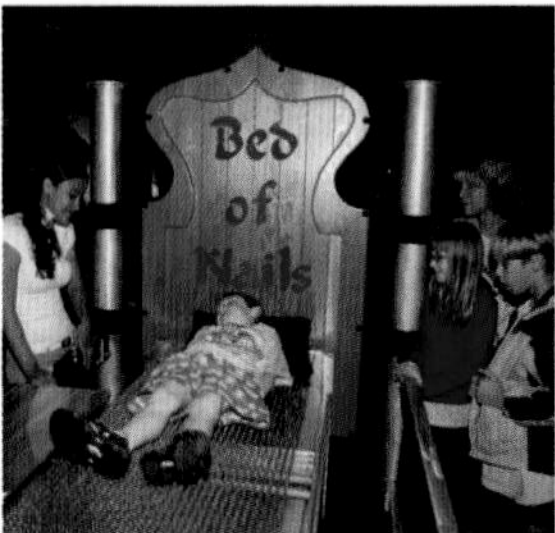

THE BASICS

www.wonderworksonline.com

G4

Pointe Orlando, 9067 International Drive, Exit 74A

407/351-8800

Daily 9am–midnight

Café

Lynx routes 8, 38 and 42; I-Ride

Very good

Moderate (laser tag extra, inexpensive)

HIGHLIGHTS

- Bubble Lab
- MindBall
- Bed of nails
- Velocity Ball
- Earthquake Experience
- Wonder Coasters
- Space Shuttle simulation

A secret science lab was torn from its site by a tornado and landed upside down on International Drive. The hundreds of experiments inside are still in perfect working condition, waiting for you—the scientists—to try them out.

Welcome The gateway into Wonderworks sets the scene for the rest of the crazy, mind-boggling attraction. An inversion tunnel turns what should be a straightforward 10ft (3m) walk into a fight between mind and body. You know that it's just a matter of putting one foot in front of the other, but your eyes fool your mind into thinking you are falling and you end up clinging to the side rail.

High-tech hardware Wonderworks finds lots of fun ways to showcase technology. MindBall uses your own brain waves to move a ball invisibly across a table, while Space Shuttle simulation enables you to re-enter the atmosphere and attempt a landing at Cape Canaveral while keeping your feet firmly on the ground. You can also try on the replica astronaut suit just like the ones worn by shuttle crews when they need to do work outside their spacecraft. Back on earth, experience what it feels like to be on the receiving end of an earthquake measuring 5.3 on the Richter scale. Younger children will particularly love the Bubble Lab where they can make bubbles as big as they are, but taller kids will make a bee line for the Wonder Coasters, where they can virtually design and test their own roller coaster. For something a little different, try lying on the bed of nails.

International Drive

With lots of opportunities to stop and extend your day, plus numerous tempting eateries, I-Drive makes a great walking route.

DISTANCE: 4 miles (6.5km) **ALLOW:** 3 hours, not including visits

START

POINTE ORLANDO G4
Lynx routes 8, 38, 42, 58 and 111; I-Ride

❶ Start your day at Pointe Orlando (▷ 63). Perhaps have a late breakfast at Johnny Rocket's before diving into the fun experiments at Wonderworks (▷ 66).

❷ Turn left out of Wonderworks. After passing Pirates Cove Adventure Golf, the quirky facade of Ripley's Believe It or Not (▷ 69) comes into view.

❸ Cross the intersection of Sand Lake Road, then cross to the left-hand side of International Drive. Heading north, you'll pass Titanic the Experience (▷ 69) and CSI: The Experience Orlando (▷ 68) on your left.

❹ Cross to the right-hand side of International Drive, and walk on past Magical Midway karting and arcades to Wet 'n' Wild (▷ 69).

❺ Make a final crossing to the left-hand side of International Drive where you'll find iFly Adventure indoor sky-diving center.

❻ Eventually the road sweeps to the left and you get your first views of Orlando Premium Outlets—International Drive (▷ 69). Look for the turning for Fun Spot Way on the left, which leads to Fun Spot America (▷ 68).

❼ You'll pass Bass Pro Shops Outdoor World (▷ 70) on the right, for all your outdoor clothing, camping and sporting goods needs.

❽ Only 0.2 miles (0.3km) on, you'll reach Orlando Premium Outlets—International Drive (▷ 69), the end of the walk. Get ready to shop!

END

ORLANDO PREMIUM OUTLETS—INTERNATIONAL DRIVE H2
Lynx routes 8, 24 and 42; I-Ride

More to See

AQUATICA

www.aquaticabyseaworld.com

A water park that combines rides and pools with fishy attractions. Dolphin Plunge is a water chute that travels through the dolphin habitat.

H5 5800 Water Play Way 888/800-5447 Core hours: daily 9–6; Nov to mid-Feb closed Mon–Tue; hours extended in summer and on some hols Restaurant and cafés Lynx routes 8, 38, 50 and 111; I-Ride Excellent Expensive

CSI: THE EXPERIENCE ORLANDO

orlando.csiexhibit.com

Find the clues and solve the crimes just like the famous forensics team in this walk-through attraction.

G3 7220 International Drive 407/226-7220 Mon–Sat 10–9, Sun 10–8 (last entry 45 mins before closing) Restaurants and cafés Lynx routes 8, 38 and 42; I-Ride Good Moderate

FUN SPOT AMERICA ORLANDO

This amusement park has entertainment for all ages, including the world's second tallest SkyCoaster at 250ft (76m) and White Lightning, Orlando's only wooden roller coaster.

H3 5700 International Drive 407/363-3867 Daily 2pm–midnight Cafés Lynx routes 8, 38 and 42; I-Ride Good Park admission free, access to all rides expensive

THE HOLY LAND EXPERIENCE

www.theholylandexperience.com

The Holy Land Experience brings the words of the Bible to life, re-creating the locations of the story of Christ, his miracles and his missions.

J2 4655 Vineland Road 407/872-2272 Tue–Sat 10–6 Cafés Lynx routes 24 and 40 Excellent Moderate

THE MALL AT MILLENIA

www.mallatmillenia.com

This mall has the finest upscale shopping in the city.

J2 4200 Conroy Road 407/363-3555 Mon, Thu–Sat 10–10, Tue 10–7, Wed, Sun 11–7 Restaurants and food court Lynx routes 24, 40 and 303 Excellent Free

Malls galore for the best in shopping in Orlando

Aquatica's Dolphin Plunge

ORLANDO PREMIUM OUTLETS

www.premiumoutlets.com

Two malls anchor the north and south ends of the International Drive area. South on Vineland Avenue is an open-air mall with cut-price designer items. The northern branch features many main-street names.

F6 8200 Vineland Avenue 407/238-7787 Mon–Sat 10am–11pm, Sun 10–9 Food court Lynx route 8; I-Ride Very good Free
H2 4951 International Drive 407/352-9600 Mon–Sat 10am–11pm, Sun 10–9 Food court Lynx routes 8, 24 and 42; I-Ride Very good Free

REBOUNDERZ

www.rebounderzorlando.com

This indoor trampoline center has a rebounding surface plus dodgeball and fitness programs. Bare feet are not allowed, so wear socks.

H3 6725 South Kirkman Road 407/704-6723 Mon–Thu 10–10, Fri–Sat 10–11, Sun 10–8 Lynx routes 8, 24, 42, 58 and 111; I-Ride Access good, but activities not suitable for all Moderate

RIPLEY'S BELIEVE IT OR NOT

www.ripleys.com

An "odditorium" full of weird stuff.

G4 8201 International Drive 407/345-0501 Daily 9.30am–midnight Lynx routes 8, 38 and 42; I-Ride Excellent Moderate

TITANIC THE EXPERIENCE

www.titanictheexperience.com

Explore full-scale re-creations of parts of this doomed ship with costumed guides. Dinner show Wed, Fri, Sat.

G3 7324 International Drive 407/248-1166 Jun–Jul daily 10–9, Aug 10–8, Sep–May 10–6 Food court Lynx routes 8, 24 and 42; I-Ride Very good Moderate (dinner show extra charge)

WET 'N WILD

www.wetnwildorlando.com

Some seriously thrilling water rides.

G3 6200 International Drive 407/351-1800 or 800/992-WILD Apr–Aug daily 9.30–7 (until 9 in summer); Sep–Mar daily 10–5; extended hours on some holidays Cafés Lynx routes 8, 21, 38 and 42; I-Ride Very good Expensive

Float away at Wet 'n Wild on International Drive

Shopping

AX ARMANI EXCHANGE

www.armaniexchange.com
You'll find great end-of-line items from this energetic fashion empire at this outlet store.
F6 Unit 1122, Orlando Premium Outlets Mall, 8200 Vineland Avenue 407/550-4490 Lynx route 8; I-Ride

BASS & CO

www.ghbass.com
Footwear and clothing for the family with the emphasis on comfortable fashion.
F6 Unit 900, Orlando Premium Outlets Mall, 8200 Vineland Avenue 407/238-2772 Lynx route 8; I-Ride

BASS PRO SHOPS OUTDOOR WORLD

www.basspro.com
The place for your fishing, hunting and camping supplies—you can even buy live bait from vending machines when the store is closed.
H3 5156 International Drive 407/563-5200 Lynx routes 8, 38 and 42; I-Ride

CHANEL

www.chanel.com
French couture at its best with the Coco purses and matching footwear.
J2 The Mall at Millennia, 4200 Conroy Road 407/352-5100 Lynx routes 24 and 40

DISNEY CHARACTER WAREHOUSE

Official Disney end-of-line merchandise mixed with full-price items.
H2 Suite 95, Premium Outlets Orlando, 4591 International Drive 407/354-3255 Lynx routes 8, 38 and 42; I-Ride

EDWIN WATTS GOLF

www.edwinwattsgolf.com
Everything for the rookie or experienced golfer: clubs, balls, footwear and a choice of golf apparel.
G4 7024 International Drive 407/352-2535 Lynx routes 8, 38 and 42; I-Ride

FOOT LOCKER

www.footlocker.com
A range of end-of-line and sports footwear for however you get active.
H2 Suite 77, Premium Outlets Orlando, 4591 International Drive 407/352-0804 Lynx routes 8, 38 and 42; I-Ride

THE OUTDOOR LIFE

Bass Pro Shops Outdoor World (▷ left) runs a series of workshops related to outdoor pursuits. Learn how to tie fishing flies and how to cast a rod. You can also take lessons in how to use a GPS for cross-country navigation and map reading, how to use kayaks and canoes or have a golf demo with an equipment specialist. Hunters will enjoy the "turkey hunting basics," while the rest of the family may choose a session on how to cook food on outdoor smokers and grills.

GUCCI

www.gucci.com
Italian style by one of the most famous names in fashion. The off-the-peg fashions are supported by shoes and accessories, such as the impeccable Gucci belts and bags.
J2 The Mall at Millennia, 4200 Conroy Road 407/903-1033 Lynx routes 24 and 40

JIMMY CHOO

www.jimmychoo.com
The most sought-after shoes of the last decade, Jimmy Choos make an exceptionally sexy statement and can only be found in a few outlets in the US.
J2 The Mall at Millennia, 4200 Conroy Road 407/352-6310 Lynx routes 24 and 40

LEVI'S® OUTLET STORE

Levi's denim jeans are an American icon and its range of modern styles offers something for all body shapes.
H2 Suite 112, Premium Outlets Orlando, 4591 International Drive 407/903-5412 Lynx routes 8, 38 and 42; I-Ride

NIKE

www.nike.com
Leading American sports company for serious fashion-led sportswear.
F6 Unit 600, Orlando Premium Outlets Mall, 8200 Vineland Avenue 407/239-3663 Lynx route 8; I-Ride

OFF 5TH—SAKS FIFTH AVENUE OUTLET

This upscale New York department store dispatches end-of-line and unsold seasonal stock to Premium Outlets Orlando, so you could pick up a bargain here.

H2 Suite 154, Premium Outlets Orlando, 4591 International Drive 407/354-5757 Lynx routes 8, 38 and 42; I-Ride

POLO RALPH LAUREN FACTORY STORE

www.ralphlauren.com

The relaxed "preppy" style of Ralph Lauren polo clothing for the whole family comes at a discount price here.

H2 Suite 180, Premium Outlets Orlando, 4591 International Drive 407/903-0339 Lynx routes 8, 38 and 42; I-Ride

SHEPLERS WESTERN STORE

www.sheplers.com

Stocks all your western-wear needs, from boots, jeans and shirts to chaps and hats. Also a range of theme souvenirs.

H3 5156 International Drive 407/563-1063 Lynx routes 8, 38 and 42; I-Ride

TEVA

www.teva.com

Rugged yet stylish action footwear, including their revolutionary multi-terrain sports sandals. Whether you're walking, hiking or jogging you'll find a comfortable fit here.

F6 Unit 2091, Orlando Premium Outlets Mall, Vineland Avenue 407/915-3160 Lynx route 8

THAROO & CO

www.tharooco.com

The finest jewelers on I-Drive. You'll find one-of-a-kind pieces and mainstream designs, plus collections of named brands like Mont Blanc. Come here for all your Pandora accessories.

G4 Pointe Orlando, 9101 International Drive 407/264-0200 Lynx routes 8, 38, 42, 58 and 111

TIMBERLAND

www.timberland.com

Timberland started with rugged footwear, but its growing retail empire also has clothing and outerwear that's popular throughout the world.

H2 Suite 31, Premium Outlets Orlando, 4591 International Drive 407/370-6630 Lynx routes 8, 38 and 42; I-Ride

TOMMY HILFIGER

The latest and perhaps greatest success story in American fashion, Tommy Hilfiger was born in 1951 as one of nine children. He began his retail empire with one store in his native northeast and began designing under his label "Tommy" in 1984. In 1994, performer Snoop Dogg wore a Tommy shirt during an appearance on *Saturday Night Live*, kick-starting a stellar rise in demand. Today sales of Tommy clothing top $2 billion per year and Hilfiger is a major influence on urban high-street styling in the US.

TOD'S

www.tods.com

Italian leather styling at it's best with a range of classic and fashion shoes, bags and accessories.

F6 Unit 1149, Orlando Premium Outlets Mall, Vineland Avenue 407/465-1820 Lynx route 8

TOMMY BAHAMA EMPORIUM

www.tommybahama.com

The perfect clothes and accessories for the sultry Florida climate, from swimwear to golf wear to smart casual ensembles for daytime or evenings.

G4 Pointe Orlando, 9101 International Drive 321/281-5886 Lynx routes 8, 38, 42, 50 and 111; I-Ride

TOMMY HILFIGER

www.tommy.com

Tommy Hilfiger (▷ panel) offers what he calls "classic styling with a twist," bringing the East Coast look within the price range of the average shopper.

F6 Unit 200, Orlando Premium Outlets Mall, Vineland Avenue 407/239-7488 Lynx route 8; I-Ride

Entertainment and Nightlife

BACKSTAGE
Sounds from the 1980s to the present day.
G4 Rosen Plaza Hotel, 9700 International Drive 407/996-9700 Wed–Sun 8pm–2am Lynx routes 8, 24, 42, 50 and 111; I-Ride

B.B. KING'S BLUES CLUB
www.bbkingclubs.com
Resident bands play some excellent classic tracks and there's a dance floor. You can eat here.
G4 Pointe Orlando, 9101 International Drive 407/370-4550 Fri–Sat noon–2am, Sun–Thu 12–12 Lynx routes 8, 38 and 42; I-Ride

CINEMARK FESTIVAL BAY
www.cinemark.com
Multiscreen complex showing the latest releases.
H3 5150 International Drive 800/326-3264 Showings 12–10.30 Lynx routes 8, 24 and 42; I-Ride

HOWL AT THE MOON
www.howlatthemoon.com
This live music bar encourages audiences to sing-along.
G4 8815 International Drive 407/354-5999 Fri–Sat 6–2, Sun–Thu 7–2 Lynx routes 8, 24 and 42; I-Ride

ICEBAR ORLANDO
www.icebarorlando.com
The air is kept at a chilly 27°F (2.7°C) so coats and gloves are supplied. Over 21s only after 9.30, children (8–20) may visit between 7pm and 9pm. The adjoining nightclub FIRE Lounge is the place for hot sounds.
G4 8967 International Drive 407/351-0361 Fri–Sat 7–2, Thu 7–1, Sun–Wed 7–12 Lynx routes 8, 38 and 42; I-Ride

IMPROV
www.theimprovorlando.com
The region's best stand-up venue is a showcase of comedy talent. Dinner shows available. Age 21s and over only.
G4 Pointe Orlando, 9101 International Drive 407/480-5233 Show times: Mon 6, Tue–Thu 8, Fri 8 and 10.30, Sat 7.30 and 10.15, Sun 7.30 Lynx routes 8, 24, 38, 42, 58 and 111; I-Ride

HOLLYWOOD STATISTICS

With Hollywood the major player in filmmaking, it's not surprising that a trip to the movies is one of the most popular ways to spend a Saturday night. Memorial Day in May 2013 saw over $314 million dollars spent at the box office. To date, the highest-grossing movie in American and world box offices is *Avatar*, although the film that made the most money during its first weekend was *Harry Potter and the Deathly Hallows*. What is coming next to a theater near you?

OUTTA CONTROL MAGIC SHOW
A fun family show combining eye-popping magic with comedy.
G4 Wonderworks, 9067 International Drive 407/351-8800 Show times 6pm and 8pm Lynx routes 8, 24, 38, 42, 58 and 111; I-Ride

PIRATE'S DINNER ADVENTURE
www.piratesdinneradventure.com
A swashbuckling yarn taking place around an impressive galleon set.
G3 6400 Carrier Drive 407/248-0590 or 800/866-2469 Mon–Fri 7.30, Sat–Sun 8.15 Lynx routes 8, 38 and 42; I-Ride

REGAL CINEMAS POINTE ORLANDO STADIUM 20 + IMAX
www.regmovies.com
Twenty-one separate theaters in the huge Pointe Orlando complex.
G4 Pointe Orlando, 9101 International Drive 407/248-9045 Showings 11–11 Lynx routes 8, 24, 38, 42, 58 and 111; I-Ride

SLEUTH'S MERRY MYSTERY DINNER SHOW
www.sleuths.com
When one of the audience is murdered during the meal, lend a hand to help solve the crime.
G4 8267 International Drive 407/363-1985 Nightly 7.30, other shows depending on season Lynx routes 8, 38 and 42; I-Ride

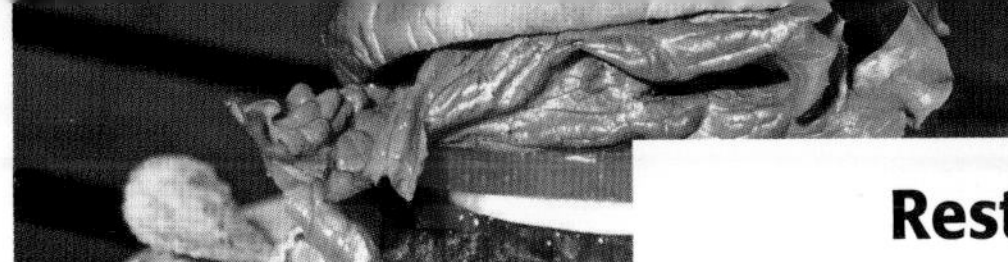

Restaurants

PRICES

Prices are approximate, based on a 3-course meal for one person.
$$$ over $60
$$ $30–$60
$ under $30

BAHAMA BREEZE ($–$$)

www.bahamabreeze.com
The Caribbean menu and live music make this a popular venue for families and a younger crowd late into the night.
G4 8849 International Drive 407/248-2499 Lunch, dinner Lynx routes 8, 38 and 42; I-Ride

B-LINE DINER ($–$$)

www.hyatt.com
A menu of old-fashioned favorites such as hot dogs and apple pie, plus modern healthy choices.
G4 Regency Hyatt Orlando, 9801 International Drive 407/284-1234 24 hours Lynx routes 8, 24, 38, 42, 58 and 111; I-Ride

CAFÉ TU TU TANGO ($$)

www.cafetututango.com
The mix-and-match menu features dishes from the Mediterranean, Caribbean, South America and the Pacific.
G4 8625 International Drive 407/248-2222 Lunch, dinner Lynx routes 8, 38 and 42; I-Ride

THE CAPITAL GRILLE ($$$)

www.thecapitalgrille.com
This fine dining restaurant places an emphasis on excellent grilled meats including aged steaks, succulent lamb and juicy duck.
G4 9101 International Drive, at Pointe Orlando 407/370-4392 Lunch, dinner Lynx routes 8, 38, 42, 50, 58 and 111; I-Ride

CHARLEY'S STEAK HOUSE ($$$)

www.talkofthetownrestaurants.com
Meat is specially selected, aged and then cut in-house and cooked over oak at this family-owned steak house.
G4 8255 International Drive 407/363-0228 Dinner Lynx routes 8, 38 and 42; I-Ride

HOW DO YOU LIKE IT?

A good steak depends on many factors, including the animal's diet, the aging process of the meat and the cut. One thing's for sure, if it's not cooked to your liking, it's going to spoil your enjoyment. Here are the terms you'll need to know.
Rare—brown exterior; raw, cold interior
Medium rare—brown exterior; warm red center
Medium—brown except for a small hot-pink interior
Medium well—no pink interior, but a little juice

THE CHEESECAKE FACTORY ($–$$)

www.thecheesecakefactory.com
This chain is renowned for its vast menu (with 50 cheesecakes) and huge portions.
G5 4200 Conroy Road (at The Mall at Millennia) 407/226-0333 Lunch, dinner Lynx routes 24 and 40

DAVE AND BUSTER'S ($–$$)

A great family eatery and sports bar. The menu is varied but based on standard steaks, burgers, pasta-type entrees and there's a good range on the kid's menu.
G4 8986 International Drive 407/541-3300 Lunch, dinner Lynx routes 8, 38, 42, 50, 58 and 111; I-Ride

DINE WITH SHAMU® ($$$)

www.seaworld.com
Watch a training session while tucking into a buffet-style meal beside the killer whale's pool. Trainers are on hand to answer questions.
G3 SeaWorld, 7007 SeaWorld Drive 407/351-3600 or 800/327-2420 11.30–5.30 depending on season Lynx routes 8, 38, 50 and 111; I-Ride

FISHBONES ($$–$$$)

With a superb selection of market-fresh fish and seafood, this is the place for lobster and Florida

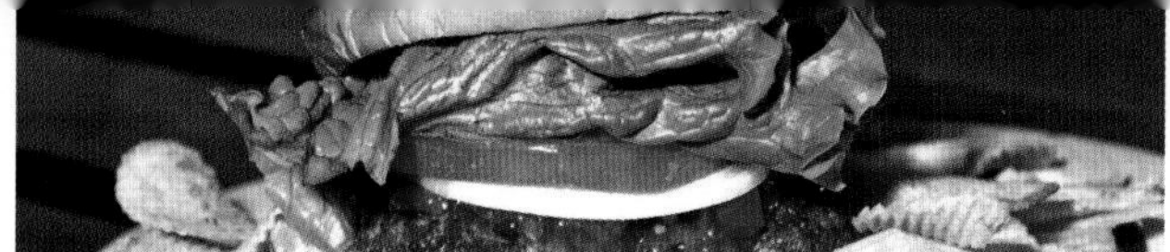

stone crab. Steaks come courtesy of Charley's (▷ 73).
G3 ✉ 6707 Sand Lake Road ☎ 407/352-0135 Dinner Lynx routes 8, 21, 38 and 42; I-Ride

GREENS AND GRILLE ($)

www.greensandgrille.com
Freshly made salads with signature salad dressings, soups and sandwiches.
J2 ✉ 4104 Millenia Boulevard, Suite 114 ☎ 407/770-1407 Lunch, dinner Lynx routes 24, 40 and 305

JOHNNY ROCKETS ($)

www.johnnyrockets.com
Sit at indoor booths or at chrome tables in this '50s-style diner. Burgers and all-day breakfasts are served to a rock-and-roll soundtrack.
J2 ✉ The Mall at Millennia, 4200 Conroy Road ☎ 407/903-1006 Breakfast, lunch, dinner Lynx routes 24 and 40

KEKE'S ($)

www.kekes.com
Keke's has a full range of sweet and savory dishes, plus delicious combos. There are several locations; this one is close to Mall of Millenia.
J2 ✉ 4192 Conroy Road ☎ 407/226-1400 Breakfast, lunch Lynx routes 24, 40 and 305

OLIVE GARDEN ($–$$)

www.olivegarden.com
The American/Italian food is always tasty here.
H1 ✉ 4101 Conroy Road ☎ 407/345-8331 Lunch, dinner Lynx routes 24 and 40

RED LOBSTER ($–$$)

www.redlobster.com
Affordable seafood and shellfish cooked any way you want it.
G3 ✉ 5936 International Drive ☎ 407/351-9313 Lunch, dinner Lynx routes 8, 38 and 42; I-Ride

ROY'S ($$–$$$)

www.roysrestaurant.com
Hawaiian fusion cuisine concentrates on fresh seafood accented by delicious sauces and marinades. The blackened *ahi* is a signature dish.
F4 ✉ 7760 West Sand Lake Road ☎ 407/352-4844 Dinner

WHAT IS FUSION FOOD?

One definition is the "integrating of disparate styles and ingredients" (Wikipedia), where culinary traditions from more than one culture or geographical region are blended. This new fashion was born as mass travel created a more informed restaurant clientele at the same time as the client base in many urban areas became more culturally diverse. Fusion cuisine was innovated in California, but soon took hold in multicultural metropolitan areas such as Miami, Vancouver (Canada) and Sydney (Australia).

SONIC ($)

www.sonicdrivein.com
Hot dogs, burgers, wraps and hot sandwiches are delivered to your table or your car.
H3 ✉ 5399 International Drive ☎ 407/352-0016 Breakfast, lunch, dinner Lynx routes 8, 38 and 42; I-Ride

TAVERNA OPA ($$)

www.opaorlando.com
A true Greek taverna with meze dishes and grilled meats, chicken and fish. Plus Greek favorites like moussaka and *baklava*.
G4 ✉ Pointe Orlando, 9101 International Drive ☎ 407/351-8660 Lunch, dinner Lynx routes 8, 24, 38, 42, 50, 58 and 111; I-Ride

TEXAS DE BRAZIL ($$)

www.texasdebrazil.com
Tuck into skewers of your favorite meat grilled to perfection at this authentic Brazilian *churrascaria* (meat restaurant).
G3 ✉ 5259 International Drive ☎ 407/355-0355 Lunch, dinner; brunch Sat–Sun at lunch Lynx routes 8, 38 and 42; I-Ride

THAI THANI ($–$$)

www.thaithani.net
Thai dishes, with the spiciness toned down for Western palates, served in a traditional dining room. If you want more heat tell your server.
H5 ✉ 11025 South International Drive ☎ 407/239-9733 Lunch, dinner Lynx route 8; I-Ride

The metro area stretches for hundreds of square miles. However, the center of Downtown Orlando is a tiny enclave with only a few high-rise buildings, with cultural sights and pleasant districts for shopping.

1
2
3
4
5
a
b
LEE
88
ORANGE
AVENUE
NORTH
Ell Street
Lake Killarne
Killarney D
FAIRBANKS
AVENUE
87
EDGEWATER
DRIVE
L Lake Fairview
Minnesota
Neptune Drive
Lake Sarah
DubsDread Golf Course
Lake Daniel
Maury Road
Par Street East
86
Avenue
Lake Silver
King Street West
King Street East
Rio Grande Avenue
Bryn Mawr Street
Winter Park Street West
Helen
PRINCETOWN
STREET
WEST
85
COLLEGE PARK
ORANGE
BLOSSOM
TRAIL
NORTH
North
New Hampshire Street West
Ivanhoe
Boulevard North
Poinsetta Avenue
Lake Ivanhoe
Antique Row
Lake Adair
Lakeview Street
84
Lake Concord
COLONIAL
DRIVE
WEST
83C
Amelia
Street
West
82B
83A
Rosalind Ave N
Orange County Regional History Center
0
1km
0
½ mile

ROAD
Webster Avenue West
Denning Drive North
Canton Avenue West
NORTH
Morse Boulevard West
Morse Boulevard East
WEST
FAIRBANKS AVENUE WEST
ORLANDO
AVENUE
NORTH
Avenue
WINTER PARK
Lake Virginia
ORANGE
AVENUE
Denning Drive South
Pennsylvania Avenue South
Mead Botanical Gardens
Lake Sue Avenue East
Nottingham Street
Lake Shore Drive
Fawsett Road
Chelton Circle
Winter Park Road
Glenridge Way
Lake Winyah
Lake Estelle
Lake Sue
Orlando Science Center
Loch Haven Park
Orlando Museum of Art
Lake Forest
Princetown St E
Loch Haven Park
Winter Park Road East
Palm Lane
Lake Rowena
Harry P Leu Gardens
Lake Formosa
Mennello Museum of American Art
Corrine Drive
Nebraska Street
Virginia Drive
Falcon Dr
Lake Cay Dee
Lake Shannon
Chelsea Street
Chelsea Street
Lake Highland Drive
Lake Highland
MILLS
AVENUE
Hampton Avenue
Bumby Avenue North
Druid Lake
Maguire Boulevard
Marks Street East
Park Lake
COLONIAL
DRIVE
EAST
Amelia Street East
Ferncreek Avenue North
Hampton Avenue North
Bumby Avenue South
Primrose Drive North
Orlando Festival Park
Eola Park
Robinson Street East
Thornton Park
Central Boulevard East
Lake Lawson
Fern Creek
Street East
Lake Olive
STREET
EAST
SOUTH
c
d
e

Harry P. Leu Gardens

Soak up the aromas of the superb roses on display in the peaceful Harry P. Leu Gardens

THE BASICS

www.leugardens.org
d3
1920 North Forest Avenue
407/246-2620
Daily 9–5, longer hours in summer
Café
Lynx route 313
Very good
Inexpensive; free first Mon of every month
Lectures, special seasonal displays throughout the year

HIGHLIGHTS

- The Camellia Garden
- The Rose Garden
- The White Garden
- The Herb Garden
- The lakeshore views
- Leu Mansion
- The xerophyte (plants that need little water) garden
- The cycads (ancient palms abundant during the Jurassic period) collection

The Leu estate is a tribute to Orlando-born Harry P. Leu who, after purchasing this 1850s farmstead, amassed a superb collection of plants to start one of America's finest tropical gardens.

The gardens The Leu estate has several botanical highlights within its 50 acres (20ha). It is home to one of the largest camellia collections on the east coast, with more than 2,000 species (best viewed between November and March) and the largest formal rose garden in Florida, containing nearly 250 varieties (a riot of color all year). You can explore the largest banana collection in the USA, a butterfly garden, and an "ideas garden" offering inspiration for Florida residents on how to work with local weather and native plants. A maze of paths meanders among these different natural environments, and the whole collection sits under a canopy of mature native oaks.

History The Leu house itself is worth exploring. Overlooking a lakeshore, the central part of the mansion was erected in 1858 by Angeline and David Mizell, who farmed cotton where the gardens now stand. The house reached its present size during the early 20th century, under the ownership of the Pell and Woodward families. Businessman Harry P. Leu bought the property in 1936. The Leus traveled extensively, bringing back plants, tubers and seeds for their growing collection. The house has been painstakingly restored to its turn-of-the-19th-century style and is listed in the National Register of Historic Places.

How food has shaped Orange County—an exhibit at the Regional History Center

TOP 25 Orange County Regional History Center

Even cities as modern and forward-looking as Orlando have a fascinating history. The Regional History Center pulls together the threads of the Central Florida story.

All rise Set in the old 1927 Orange County Courthouse in downtown, Orlando's History Center opened in 2000. There's a wealth of information here and it has been carefully and beautifully dramatized with depictions of the major lifestyles from throughout Florida's long history.

Follow the timeline The first stop on the tour is Orientation Theater. Relax in a rocker on a porch, surrounded by the sights and sounds of old and new Central Florida, then immerse yourself in Timucuan culture. These people welcomed the Spanish when they ventured inland in the 16th century, but within a few decades they were wiped out by diseases, brought by those on board the ships from Europe. Fast forward to the early 1800s and explore a Seminole settlement and Cracker home. These two peoples lived side-by-side. They were anti-establishment, proud and highly adapted to their environment. Around the campfire you'll learn how both got their names before you head into the late 1800s and find yourself surrounded by citrus groves which are still a mainstay of the Florida economy. The museum shows the background to Orlando's meteoric rise at the end of the 20th century with photographs of the construction of the Magic Kingdom® and development of the modern city.

THE BASICS

www.thehistorycenter.org
c4
65 East Central Boulevard
407/836-8500 or 800/965-2030
Mon–Sat 10–5, Sun 12–5
Lynx routes 3, 7, 11, 13, 15, 18 and 40; Lymmo
Excellent
Moderate
Program of guest speakers and special family events

HIGHLIGHTS

- Re-creation of a "cracker" homestead
- Photographs taken during the building of the Magic Kingdom®
- Walk through dioramas of the citrus industry

Orlando Museum of Art

One of the top art museums in Florida—the excellent Orlando Museum of Art

THE BASICS

www.omart.org
c3
2416 North Mills Avenue, I-4 to Exit 85, head east
407/896-4231
Tue–Fri 10–4, Sat–Sun 12–4
Lynx route 125
Excellent
Inexpensive
Gallery tours and lectures

HIGHLIGHTS

- Avian Pendant: gold jewelry from Costa Rica dating to AD1000–1500
- Ornate religious carving of the Zatopec peoples (cAD300–600) from Oaxaca, Mexico
- The Sun Vow: a bronze by Hermon Atkins MacNeil (c1901)
- Ceremonial Zulu wedding cape from southern Africa

The Orlando Museum of Art's reputation is founded on its American tribal artifacts. It also exhibits varied post-Independence art and a fascinating collection of Native African crafts.

American Art This eclectic collection covers the full range of American history and comprises paintings, prints, drawings, photos and sculpture. Notable artists include John Singer Sargent, Georgia O'Keeffe—one of the 20th century's most influential women artists—and Ansel Adams, founding father of landscape photography.

Ancient American Art Collection The Art of the Ancient Americas Collection is now the best in the southern US, boosted by impressive donations by Dr. Solomon D. Klotz and his artist wife Harriet Klotz, who amassed a large collection during their married life. Over 30 different cultural groups are represented from throughout North, South and Central America and artifacts range in date from 2000BC to 1521. The collection is strong in artifacts of the Pueblo cultures of the American Southwest, the Anasazi of the southern Colorado Plateau, and their close relatives, the Mogollon of the high Chihuahuan Desert.

African Art Collection This is an excellent collection of ceremonial and everyday artifacts from various parts of Africa, including intricate Zulu and Xhosa beadwork and basketware. The most interesting objects belong to the Dogon and their fascinating funerary and death rituals.

Get into science with a hands-on approach at the Orlando Science Center

TOP 25

Orlando Science Center

The aim of the Orlando Science Center is to help all age groups understand complicated theories. It's hands-on learning, with exhibits designed with the help of theme park "imagineers."

Make science fun Many of the exhibits are linked to science curricula at various grades, so you can assess suitability for age groups. Kids Town is perfect for preschoolers as the world is shrunk to their own size. The Water Table is a hands-on exploration of how we deal with our important natural resources: Kids can build dams to collect rainwater and canals to distribute it. NatureWorks' exhibits are based around our natural world: The ecosystem of natural Florida is recreated in microcosm with its shallow mangrove swampland, scrub, coasts and forests.

Moving on Other areas explore the scientific principles that govern our physical world. Exhibits are more suited to older children and adults. Our Planet, Our Universe explains some of the most mysterious forces that shape the Earth and the solar system. The Dr. Phillips CineDome has one of the world's largest Iwerks domed screens, where films are projected all around the audience.

Serious science You'll find the region's only public-access electron microscope here, and Florida's largest public-access refractor telescope is at the Crosby Observatory, allowing amateur astronomers the chance to observe stars, moons and planets.

THE BASICS

www.osc.org
c3
777 East Princeton Street
407/514-2000
Thu–Tue 10–5
Café
Lynx route 125
Excellent
Moderate
Guest lectures. Monthly schedule of events

HIGHLIGHTS

- The Dr. Phillips CineDome
- Kids Town
- Crosby Observatory
- NatureWorks
- Our Planet, Our Universe

Winter Park

TOP 25

Rollins College (left) is at the center of the smart Winter Park district of Orlando

THE BASICS

 d2
151 West Lyman Avenue
Welcome Center 407/644-8281
Cafés, restaurants
Lynx routes 1, 9, 23, 102 and 443
Amtrak station
Free

Albin Polasek Museum
633 Osceola Avenue
407/647-6294
Tue–Sat 9.30–4, Sun 1–4
Museum inexpensive, gardens free. Guided tour included in ticket price

Charles Hosmer Morse Museum of American Art
445 North Park Avenue
407/645-5311
Tue–Sat 9.30–4, Sun 1–4 (also Fri 4–8 Nov–Apr)
Inexpensive

Cornell Museum of Fine Arts
1000 Holt Avenue
407/646-2526
Tue–Sat 10–4, Sun 12–5 (also Fri 4–8 Nov–Apr)
Free

HIGHLIGHTS

- Kraft Azalea Gardens
- Charles Hosmer Morse Museum of American Art
- Cornell Museum of Fine Arts
- Scenic boat tour

The most urbane of Orlando's suburbs, Winter Park makes a refreshing departure from the theme parks, especially for those in search of some culture.

Foundations Winter Park was founded by David Mizell in 1858. The arrival of the railroad in 1882 sealed the success of the settlement. Rollins College, established in 1885, quickly became an academic center of excellence. Early in the 20th century, when northerners would come to enjoy the temperate winters, the largest hotel in Florida was built here. Today, Winter Park is a desirable address, with great shopping on Park Avenue.

Museums The Charles Hosmer Morse Museum of American Art houses one of the most comprehensive collections of Tiffany anywhere. Most people are aware of the ornate lamps of Louis Comfort Tiffany (1848–1933), but the varied collection also includes the interior of a neo-Byzantine chapel, designed by the artist for the World's Exposition in 1893. Moravian-born sculptor Albin Polasek spent his retirement at his 3-acre (1.2ha) estate close by. His work is scattered around the grounds and the villa is decorated with Polasek's own art collection. At Rollins College, the Cornell Museum of Fine Arts has the oldest fine art collection in the state, comprising European and American paintings and sculpture.

Scenic boat tour A leisurely one-hour tour operates daily and passes lakeside mansions, Rollins College and the Kraft Azalea Gardens.

More to See

ANTIQUE ROW

Orlando's quirky quarter of collectibles and antiques stores stretches along North Orange Avenue from Colonial Drive to Lake Ivanhoe. There are bargains too, and some nice coffee shops for relaxation.

c3 Lynx route 102

EOLA PARK

A stroll around Lake Eola is the place to meet Orlando suburbanites. They'll be jogging or walking their dogs. In summer concerts take place in the small arena, and there are gondola rides on the lake.

c4 Downtown, corner of Robinson Street, Rosalind Avenue, Central Boulevard and Summerlin Avenue Open 24 hours Lynx routes 3, 7, 11, 13, 15, 18, 51 and 125; Lymmo Good Free

LOCH HAVEN PARK

This beautifully landscaped parkland surrounded by small lakes plays host to a range of cultural organizations including the Orlando Museum of Art (▷ 80), Orlando Science Center (▷ 81), the Tupperware and Shakespeare Theaters, and the Mennello Museum of American Art.

c3 East Princeton Street Cafés at Science Center Lynx route 125

MENNELLO MUSEUM OF AMERICAN ART

www.mennellomuseum.org

The Mennello Museum holds the world's preeminent collection of works by Earl Cunningham (1893–1977) and temporary exhibitions.

c3 900 East Princeton Street C407/246-4278 Tue–Sat 10.30–4.30, Sun 12–4.30 Lynx route 125 Excellent Inexpensive

THORNTON PARK

Downtown Orlando's most characterful district is a tiny enclave of cobblestone lanes with early-20th-century clapboard bungalows that mimic the original "cracker" style. It's a popular upscale residential area with shops.

c4 Cafés and restaurants Lynx routes 15, 125 and 313

Away from the razzmatazz at tranquil Lake Eola

Winter Park

A compact little neighborhood, and the prettiest in Orlando, Winter Park (▷ 82) has many attractions and is a lovely area to take a stroll.

DISTANCE: 1 mile (1.5km) **ALLOW:** 3.5 hours

START

CHARLES HOSMER MORSE MUSEUM

c2 Lynx routes 1, 9 and 23

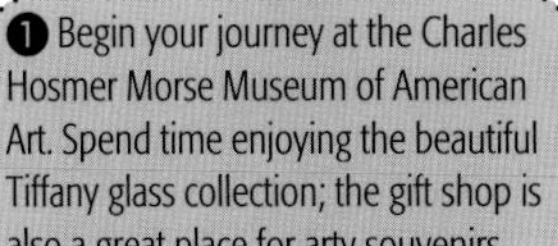

❶ Begin your journey at the Charles Hosmer Morse Museum of American Art. Spend time enjoying the beautiful Tiffany glass collection; the gift shop is also a great place for arty souvenirs.

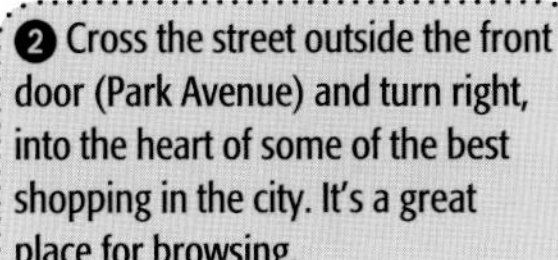

❷ Cross the street outside the front door (Park Avenue) and turn right, into the heart of some of the best shopping in the city. It's a great place for browsing.

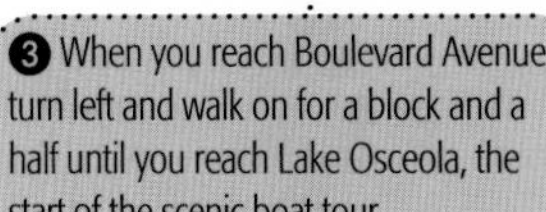

❸ When you reach Boulevard Avenue turn left and walk on for a block and a half until you reach Lake Osceola, the start of the scenic boat tour.

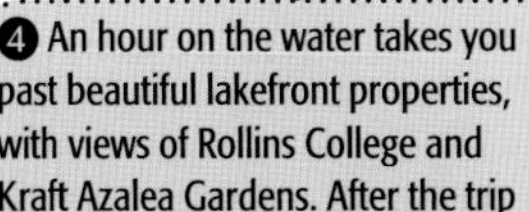

❹ An hour on the water takes you past beautiful lakefront properties, with views of Rollins College and Kraft Azalea Gardens. After the trip retrace your steps to Park Avenue.

❺ Continue your journey south (turn left at the intersection).

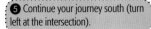

❻ On the right-hand side is Central Park. Continue south past the Park Plaza Hotel and 310 Park South (you may want to peruse the menu for a late lunch or early dinner) until you reach Holt Avenue.

❼ Turn left here onto the campus of Rollins College, famed for its Italianate styling and formal gardens. Stay on Holt Avenue to visit Knowles Chapel, venue for the concerts of the Bach Festival, before moving on to the Cornell Museum of Fine Arts.

❽ The museum has the oldest such collection in Florida, with pieces as diverse as painting from the Rubens School and sculptures by Henry Moore.

END

CORNELL MUSEUM OF FINE ARTS

c2 Lynx routes 1, 9 and 23

Shopping

A & T ANTIQUES

www.aandtfurnitureantiquesorlandofl.com

One of the oldest established stores along Antiques Row. There's a huge inventory, with pieces large and small, including a vast amount of period stained glass.

c3 · 1620 North Orange Avenue · 407/896-9831 · Lynx route 102

THE BLACK SHEEP

www.theblacksheepshop.com

Fantastic repository for lovers of needlecraft, with a vast range of silks, threads and wools, patterns and books. Also offers instruction.

d2 · 1322 North Mills Avenue · 407/894-0444 · Lynx routes 102 and 443

THE CITY ARTS FACTORY

www.cityartsfactory.com

A creative multifunction space in the downtown core where you'll find a glass-blowing artist, modern gallery and Keine/Quigley community gallery.

c5 · 29 South Orange Avenue · 407/648-7060 · Lynx routes 3, 7, 11, 13, 18 and 51

LEU GARDENS

www.leugardens.org

A veritable treasure trove for the keen gardener, including books, small tools and themed ornaments and collectibles.

d3 · 1920 North Forest Avenue · 407/246-2620 · Lynx route 313

MORSE MUSEUM

www.morsemuseum.org

A good range of Tiffany and Arts and Crafts copies, plus prints and miniatures. Books on artistic styles and genres and gifts such as picture frames and jewelry are also available.

d2 · 445 Park Avenue North, Winter Park · 407/645-5316 · Lynx routes 1, 9, 23, 102 and 443

ORLANDO MUSEUM OF ART

www.omart.org

Find books, prints and copies of objets d'art in this gift shop. Many items reflect the exhibits.

c3 · 2416 North Mills Avenue · 407/896-4231 · Lynx route 125

SOMETHING MORSE

Louis Comfort Tiffany, son of a silversmith, trained as an artist and developed an interest in the chemistry of glass. In 1881, he patented a glass that amalgamated several colors to produce myriad hues. By 1885, he was producing his signature pieces. His primary source of inspiration was nature; hence his lamps reveal a metal stem with a shade of glass leaves and blossoms. Tiffany was one of the first American artists to reach a worldwide audience. He was particularly appreciated in Paris during the art nouveau era.

ORLANDO SCIENCE CENTER

www.osc.org

Gift shop with affordable educational games.

c3 · 777 East Princeton Street · 407/514-2000 · Lynx route 125

SCOTT LAURENT COLLECTION

www.scottlaurentcollection.com

This gallery sells what are set to be the collectibles of tomorrow.

d2 · 348 Park Avenue North, Winter Park · 407/629-0278 · Lynx routes 1, 9, 23, 102 and 443

TIMOTHY'S GALLERY

www.timothysgallery.com

Over 300 artists and crafts people from across the US are represented here.

d4 · 236 Park Avenue North, Winter Park · 407/629-0707 · Lynx routes 1, 9, 12, 102 and 443

WILLIAMS-SONOMA

www.williams-sonoma.com

Excellent shop selling "kitchenalia," including gadgets, crockery, linens and cooking accessories.

d2 · 142 Park Avenue, Winter Park · 407/628-5900 · Lynx routes 1, 9, 23, 102 and 443

ZOU ZOU BOUTIQUE

www.zouzouboutique.com

This is where young socialites come to buy their evening gowns.

c4 · 2 North Summerlin Avenue, Thornton Park · 407/843-3373 · Lynx routes 15, 125 and 313

Entertainment and Nightlife

AMWAY CENTER
www.amwaycenter.com
Orlando's mega-stadium plays host to major sports events, concerts and spectacles. It's home to Orlando Magic basketball team. Range of eateries and entertainments.
b4 400 West Church Street Box office: 800/745-3000 Box office: Mon–Fri 9–6 Lynx routes 20 and 36; Lymmo

CHILLERS
www.churchstreetbars.com
Home of the best frozen daiquiris in the city, this is one of Orlando's most popular night-clubs.
c4 33 West Church Street 407/649-4270 Daily 4.30pm–2am Lynx routes 20, 36 and 40; Lymmo

DR. PHILLIPS CENTER FOR THE PERFORMING ARTS
www.drphillipscenter.org
This is the dazzling jewel in the crown of Orlando's arts scene. Downtown has been transformed in the form of this magnificent glass-sided freeform space that plays host to resident and touring companies.
c5 455 South Orange Avenue 407/839-0119 Performances throughout the year Lynx routes 7, 11, 13, 15 and 18; Lymmo

LATITUDES
www.churchstreetbars. com
A popular roof-top bar in the downtown area. It turns into an evening venue, playing the latest chart sounds.
c4 33 West Church Street 407/649-4270 Mon–Wed 3pm–10pm, Thu–Sun 3pm–2am Lynx routes 20, 36 and 40; Lymmo

MAD COW THEATRE
www.madcowtheatre.com
This award-winning, avant garde company provides thought-provoking plays.
b4 54 West Church Street 407/297-8788 Through the year Lynx route 20; Lymmo

ORLANDO BALLET
www.orlandoballet.org
Orlando's ballet company performs classical and modern ballets.
b4 Bob Car Performing Arts Center, 401 West Livingston Street 407/426-1733 Oct–May Lynx route 8; Lymmo

ORLANDO REPERTORY THEATER
www.orlandorep.com
Run in conjunction with the University of Central Florida, the Rep offers a varied schedule from drama to comedy.
c3 1001 East Princetown Street 407/896-7365 Ticket office: Mon–Fri 9–5 Lynx route 125

IS THAT REALLY YOU?
The legal age for drinking alcohol in the USA is 21 and this is stringently enforced. If you are 21–25, or are of legal age but look younger, always carry photo ID with you to enjoy a refreshing glass of beer or wine with dinner, or at a bar or club.

REGAL WINTER PARK STADIUM
www.regmovies.com
Multiscreen complex near the center of Winter Park.
c2 510 North Orlando Avenue, Winter Park 407/628-0035 Showings 12–11pm Lynx routes 1 and 9

ROLLINS COLLEGE
An annual program of dance, music, theater and film. The Bach Festival concerts take place here.
d2 1000 Holt Avenue, Winter Park 407/646-2000 Throughout the year Lynx routes 1, 9 and 102

SHINE
www.wallstplaza.net
Nightclub in this popular entertainment district. Serves signature flavored moonshines from the tap.
c4 25 Wall Street 407/849-9904 Tue, Thu 8pm–2am, Fri 4pm–2am, Sat–Sun 11am–2am Lynx routes 3, 7, 11, 13, 15 and 18; Lymmo

THE SOCIAL
www.thesocial.org
Bands at Orlando's top downtown live music venue cover all genres of popular music. Over 21s.
c4 54 North Orange Avenue 407/246-1419 Doors open 9pm Lynx routes 3, 6, 7, 11, 13, 18 and 51

Restaurants

PRICES

Prices are approximate, based on a 3-course meal for one person.

$$$ over $60
$$ $30–$60
$ under $30

AUSTIN'S COFFEE ($)
www.austincoffee.com
Voted the best café in Orlando, everything is so fresh. Also a full schedule of improv.
d2 929 West Fairbanks Avenue, Winter Park 407/975-3364 Breakfast, lunch, dinner Lynx routes 1, 9 and 16

LA BOHEME ($$$)
Refined European and North American dishes are served here. Sunday's Jazz Brunch is a downtown institution.
c5 Westin Grand Bohemian Hotel, 325 South Orange Avenue 407/313-9000 Daily dinner, Sun brunch Lynx routes 3, 6, 7, 11, 13, 18 and 51; Lymmo

BRIO TUSCAN GRILLE AND BAKERY ($$)
www.brioitalian.com
An up-to-date twist on an Italian trattoria, Brio serves great bread and some excellent pizza, as well as pasta, seafood and steaks. There's a pleasant terrace for eating alfresco.
c2 Winter Park Village, Orange Avenue, Winter Park 407/622-5611 Lunch, dinner Lynx routes 1, 9, 14, 39 and 102

BUBBALOU'S BODACIOUS BAR-B-QUE ($)
www.bubbalous.com
The place to sample barbecued meats and ribs or the mighty hot sandwiches (▷ panel).
b1 1471 Lee Road, Winter Park 407/423-1212 Lunch, dinner

CEVICHE ($–$$)
www.ceviche.com
An excellent range of tapas, ceviche (marinated raw fish) and other original dishes are on the menu at this Spanish restaurant/bar. Live flamenco performances Thu–Sat.
c4 125 West Church Street 321/281-8140 Tue–Sat dinner Lynx route 20; Lymmo

DEXTERS ($$)
www.dexwine.com
Long-established bar and diner-style eatery in the heart of Thornton Park. Sister establishment in Winter Park.
c4 808 Washington Street, Thornton Park 407/648-2777 Lunch, dinner Lynx routes 15, 125 and 313

BBQ TREAT

Voted best BBQ restaurant in 2004, 2005 and 2006 by readers of the *Orlando Weekly,* Bubbalou's Bodacious (▷ above) has genuine southern dishes and sides on its menu. Try the catfish, pulled pork, collard greens, okra and corn bread washed down with root beer or Dr. Pepper.

HILLSTONE ($$–$$$)
Enjoy renowned service and a delicious contemporary American menu at this restaurant which overlooks Lake Killarney.
d2 215 South Orlando Avenue 407/470-4005 Lunch, dinner Lynx routes 102 and 443

KRES ($$–$$$)
www.kresrestaurant.com
Contemporary urban styling and great steaks draw a mainly young urban clientele. Popular lounge in the evenings.
c4 17 West Church Street 407/409-7227 Mon–Fri lunch, dinner, Sat dinner Lynx route 20; Lymmo

LUMA ON PARK ($$)
www.lumaonpark.com
An upscale contemporary American lounge and restaurant. The daily specials reflect what's market fresh.
d2 290 South Park Avenue, Winter Park 407/599-4111 Dinner Lynx routes 102 and 443

THE RAVENOUS PIG ($–$$)
www.theravenouspig.com
This gastro-pub has had excellent reviews since it opened. The menu changes, but the monthly pig roast is popular.
d2 1234 North Orange Avenue 407/628-2333 Tue–Sat lunch, dinner Lynx route 102

Many important and popular attractions lie within a couple of hours' drive of Orlando. Choose from the natural wonders of the Florida landscape to the hi-tech world of the space race and yet more theme parks.

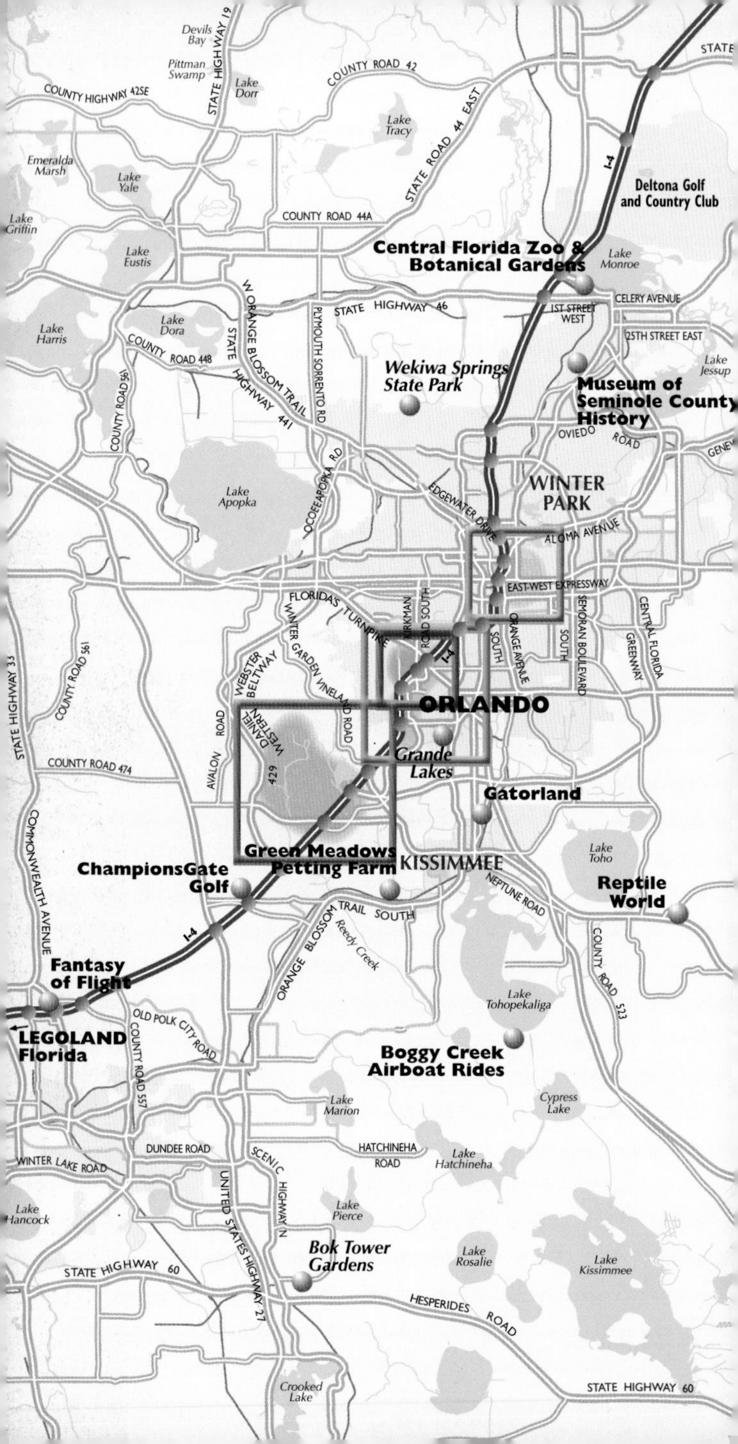

Central Florida Zoo & Botanical Gardens
Deltona Golf and Country Club
Wekiwa Springs State Park
Museum of Seminole County History
WINTER PARK
ORLANDO
Grande Lakes
Gatorland
KISSIMMEE
Green Meadows Petting Farm
ChampionsGate Golf
Reptile World
Fantasy of Flight
LEGOLAND Florida
Boggy Creek Airboat Rides
Bok Tower Gardens
I-4
Devils Bay
Pittman Swamp
Lake Dorr
Lake Tracy
Emeralda Marsh
Lake Yale
Lake Griffin
Lake Eustis
Lake Monroe
Lake Dora
Lake Harris
Lake Jessup
Lake Apopka
Lake Toho
Lake Tohopekaliga
Lake Marion
Cypress Lake
Lake Hatchineha
Lake Hancock
Lake Pierce
Lake Rosalie
Lake Kissimmee
Crooked Lake
Reedy Creek
COUNTY HIGHWAY 42SE
STATE HIGHWAY 19
COUNTY ROAD 42
STATE ROAD 44 EAST
COUNTY ROAD 44A
W ORANGE BLOSSOM TRAIL
STATE HIGHWAY 441
PLYMOUTH SORRENTO RD
STATE HIGHWAY 46
CELERY AVENUE
1ST STREET WEST
25TH STREET EAST
COUNTY ROAD 448
COUNTY ROAD 561
OCOEEAPOPKA RD
OVIEDO ROAD
EDGEWATER DRIVE
ALOMA AVENUE
EAST-WEST EXPRESSWAY
FLORIDA'S TURNPIKE
KIRKMAN ROAD SOUTH
SOUTH ORANGE AVENUE
SEMORAN BOULEVARD SOUTH
CENTRAL FLORIDA GREENWAY
WINTER GARDEN VINELAND ROAD
WEBSTER BELTWAY
DANIEL WESTERN 429
AVALON ROAD
STATE HIGHWAY 33
COUNTY ROAD 474
COMMONWEALTH AVENUE
NEPTUNE ROAD
ORANGE BLOSSOM TRAIL SOUTH
COUNTY ROAD 523
OLD POLK CITY ROAD
COUNTY ROAD 557
DUNDEE ROAD
WINTER LAKE ROAD
HATCHINEHA ROAD
SCENIC HIGHWAY N
UNITED STATES HIGHWAY 27
STATE HIGHWAY 60
HESPERIDES ROAD

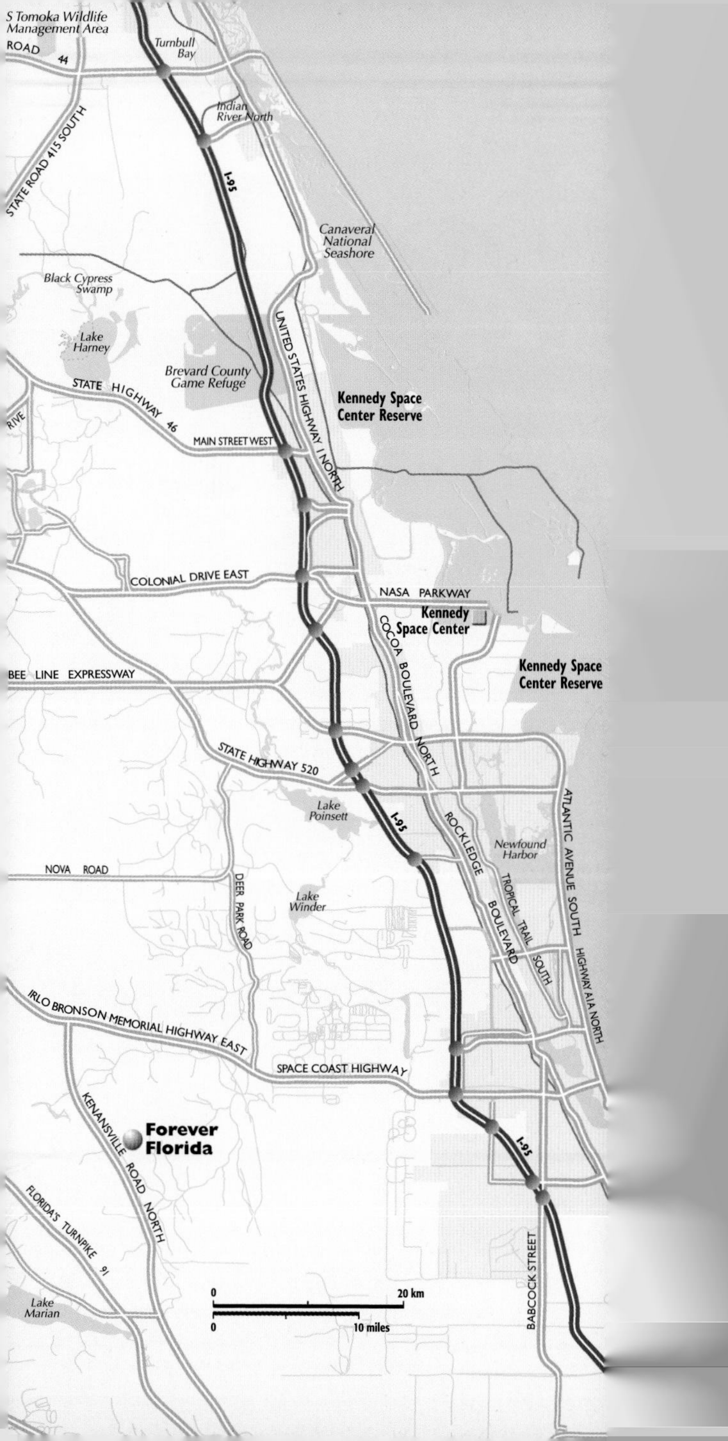

S Tomoka Wildlife Management Area
ROAD 44
Turnbull Bay
Indian River North
STATE ROAD 415 SOUTH
I-95
Canaveral National Seashore
Black Cypress Swamp
Lake Harney
Brevard County Game Refuge
UNITED STATES HIGHWAY 1 NORTH
Kennedy Space Center Reserve
STATE HIGHWAY 46
RIVE
MAIN STREET WEST
COLONIAL DRIVE EAST
NASA PARKWAY
Kennedy Space Center
COCOA BOULEVARD NORTH
BEE LINE EXPRESSWAY
Kennedy Space Center Reserve
STATE HIGHWAY 520
Lake Poinsett
I-95
ROCKLEDGE BOULEVARD
Newfound Harbor
ATLANTIC AVENUE SOUTH
NOVA ROAD
DEER PARK ROAD
Lake Winder
TROPICAL TRAIL SOUTH
HIGHWAY A1A NORTH
IRLO BRONSON MEMORIAL HIGHWAY EAST
SPACE COAST HIGHWAY
KENANSVILLE ROAD NORTH
Forever Florida
I-95
FLORIDA'S TURNPIKE 91
BABCOCK STREET
Lake Marian
0
20 km
0
10 miles

Boggy Creek Airboat Rides

Get closer to nature and take a trip with the Boggy Creek Airboat Rides company

THE BASICS

www.bcairboats.com
Off map at G9
2001 East Southport Road, Kissimmee
407/344-9550
Daily, tours every half hour 9–5 with longer days during major holidays. Reservations required for night tours
Restaurant
Good
Day tours moderate, night tours expensive

HIGHLIGHTS

- Riding on the airboat
- Seeing alligators in a natural habitat
- Pristine lakeland scenery
- Huge variety of other wildlife

On one of the most exhilarating rides in Orlando, yet you never get off the ground. It's your chance to play "crocodile hunter," but we don't advise jumping out of the boat like Crocodile Dundee!

How? The airboat is the perfect vehicle for the central Florida landscape and its numerous lakes and swamps. With the engine above water and a shallow draft, it can glide over the vast grass banks that grow around the shallows. With the engine idling, it floats almost silently to get you closer to the wildlife. The US Coast Guard accre-dited Master Captains expertly guide you to watch natural behavior in an unspoiled environment.

Where? West Lake Toho is an unspoiled and rich environment, which is a breeding ground for a diverse range of animals. It's estimated that there are hundreds of alligators of all shapes and sizes, plus turtles, snakes and birds such as bald eagles, herons, ospreys, anhingas, egrets and Sand Hill cranes.

When? Boggy Creek runs both day and night tours from two locations. Day tours last 30 minutes and take in a range of wildlife, although there's no guarantee that you'll spot alligators, as they often retreat to remote areas, especially in the middle of the day. Night tours lasting one hour are better for alligator spotting, as the animals are more active after dark. The spotlight on your captain's helmet will reflect alligators' eyes, however seeing other creatures is less likely in the dark.

Whether it's reptiles or baby elephants—you can see a wide range of creatures at the zoo

TOP 25

Central Florida Zoo & Botanical Gardens

To the northeast of Orlando, in Sanford, the Central Florida Zoo & Botanical Gardens aims to educate visitors about its collection of creatures and is committed to protecting endangered species.

A short history First established as the Sanford Zoo in the 1920s, the Central Florida Zoological Park began with a disparate collection of animals donated by traveling circuses and private owners. Today, as an accredited member of the American Zoo and Aquarium Association, it is a key player in the campaign to maximize the captive populations of several endangered species.

Animals The big cats, including two cheetahs and a breeding pair of clouded leopards, are the highlight of the collection. Siamang apes and howler monkeys are among the zoo's apes and monkeys, while a playful family of endangered red-ruffed lemurs are representative of the smaller mammals. The Herpetarium is the finest captive snake habitat in the city; see eyelash vipers, gila monsters and eastern diamondback rattlesnakes.

Habitat The zoo's home is prime Florida wetland, a great natural environment for the animals. Exhibits that make the most of the location include the Butterfly Garden and Florida Trek, which leads into the margins of the wetland. The Wharton-Smith Inc. Tropical Splash Ground is a playground with pools and fountains where kids can cool off after the animal tour.

THE BASICS

www.centralfloridazoo.org

Off map at c2

3755 N US Highway 17-92, Sanford

407/323-4450

Daily 9–5

Café

Very good

Inexpensive

Special events and lectures during the year

HIGHLIGHTS

- Clouded leopards
- Amur leopards
- Herpetarium
- Lemurs

Gatorland

TOP 25

You may need to look twice to realize you are not in Jurassic Park—these are the real thing

THE BASICS

www.gatorland.com
K8
4501 South Orange Blossom Trail
800/393-5297
Daily 10–5
Café
Lynx route 4
Good
Moderate

DID YOU KNOW?

- The name alligator comes from the Spanish "el lagarto" or "the lizard."
- In the 1960s, the American alligator was an endangered species.
- Today there are hundreds of thousands of wild 'gators in Florida alone.
- They lose their appetites when the temperature drops below 80ºF (27ºC) and can go for months without food.
- Alligators build elaborate nests and lay eggs.
- The temperature of the egg in the nest decides the sex of a baby alligator.

Gatorland is the best place to get close to Florida's most enigmatic creature, the American alligator, a species unchanged for millions of years.

Denizens of the swamps Younger children aren't always convinced that these huge monsters are real, but don't be deceived by the statuelike demeanor of the hundreds of basking adult alligators on show here. This species can move at lightning speed over short distances. Alligators and crocodiles are cold-blooded creatures and need heat to raise their body temperature to get active, so the huge adults—up to 15ft (4.5m) in length—spend much of their time inert and soaking up the sun. The only time there's any real movement is at show time, when the hunks of meat dangled temptingly a few feet above those leathery snouts cause a frenzy of snapping jaws.

The new generation Younger, and decidedly cuter alligators and hatchlings bask in smaller enclosures, often piled one atop another to reach the hottest spot. Behind the pens, a verdant tropical waterhole plays host to a number of breeding pairs, observable from a boardwalk.

Want more adventure? Gatorland offers high-adrenaline gator-related activities. The Screamin' Gator Zip Line is a 1,200ft (365m) rope experience, shooting you over crocodile pools and the Alligator Breeding Marsh. Or get down in the sand at the Rookie Wrestling pit where you can straddle your own gator, under expert guidance of course!

When you want a rest from theme parks, paddle your own canoe down the Wekiwa River

TOP 25

Wekiwa Springs State Park

Wekiwa (the Creek Native word for "spring") is a 7,800-acre (3,156ha) safe haven for a host of indigenous wildlife. The pristine landscape has changed little over the millennia.

Environment More than 700 freshwater springs issue from the Florida substrate and these are invaluable in maintaining the natural wetland environment. The main spring here spews out 42 million gallons (195 million liters) of water per day that flow north as the Wekiwa River. Within the park, 19 separate habitats, ranging from freshwater swamps at the lower levels up through pine flatwoods and hammock forests to dry sandy ridges, offer more diversity than any other park in the state and support a wealth of wildlife. Seventy-three plant species provide protection to important bird populations, including 34 species of warbler. Common animal species include raccoons, armadillo, opossum and turtles, while rarer animals for whom Wekiwa acts as a lifeline include the southern black bear, bobcat, bald eagle, gray fox and Florida mouse, a rodent found only in this state.

Access A boardwalk skirts the southern stretches of wetland, hiking trails lead into the higher woodland, and in summer you can go horse riding. But perhaps the most exciting way to enjoy the park is by canoe. From the rental dock close to the spring you can head out into the Wekiwa River, bordered by a vast natural swampland where you can imagine yourself in the Florida of yesteryear.

THE BASICS

www.floridastateparks.org

Off map at c2

1800 Wekiwa Circle, Apopka (I-4 east to Exit 94, left to Wekiwa Springs Road, turn right, drive 4 miles/6km to park entrance on right)

407/884-2008

Daily 8am–sunset

Few

Per vehicle: inexpensive

Only 300 vehicles are allowed into the park, so arrive early on holidays and summer weekends. Guided talks and open days in summer

HIGHLIGHTS

- Kayaking on the Wekiwa River
- Swimming in the freshwater spring
- Hiking in the wilderness

More to See

BOK TOWER GARDENS

www.boksanctuary.org

Author Edward W. Bok (1863–1930) bought this land as a sanctuary and gave it to the American people on his death. Frederick Law Olmsted Jr. designed the gardens in the 1920s. A 205ft (62m) neo-Gothic carillon offers daily bell ringing (1pm and 3pm), and you can visit Pinewood Estate, the neighboring home of early 20th-century industrialist C. Austin Buck.

Off map at C9 1151 Tower Boulevard, Lake Waters 863/676-1408 Daily 8–6, last ticket at 5 Café Good Moderate

CHAMPIONSGATE GOLF

www.championsgategolf.com

ChampionsGate has two renowned Greg Norman-designed courses. The International is a British-style links course. Featured in many golfing "best of" surveys, it's the home of the David Leadbetter Golf Academy. The National course curves through strands of citrus groves.

Off map at C9 1400 Masters Boulevard 407/787-4653 Tee times sunrise until 90 mins before sunset Restaurant Excellent Very expensive

FANTASY OF FLIGHT

www.fantasyofflight.com

The world's largest private collection of aircraft is the passion of aerobatic ace Kermit Weeks. Dioramas depict the history of flight and you can tour the hangers and take a trip in a bi-plane. The Sight and Sound Immersion Experiences relive the early days of flight.

Off map at C9 1400 Broadway Boulevard, S.E. Polk City 863/984-3500 Thu–Sun 10–5 Café Excellent Expensive

FOREVER FLORIDA

www.foreverflorida.com

Step into nature at this ranch and nature reserve where traditional ranching mixes with eco activities such as trails on horseback and land and everglades tours by boat or motor vehicle.

Plenty of opportunities to practice your putting

A splendid bell tower rising above Bok Tower Gardens

Off map at G9 4755 Kenansville Road, Holopaw 407/957-9794 Daily, reservations suggested Restaurant Good Varies with activities

GRANDE LAKES

www.grandelakes.com

This diverse 18-hole, par-72 course was designed by Greg Norman and routed through typical Florida wetland and forest environments. It culminates in the shadow of the luxurious Ritz-Carlton and Marriott hotels. There are exceptional practise areas, and the usual Ritz Carlton five-star service.

J6 4040 Central Florida Parkway 407/393-4900 Tee times 7–6 Restaurant Excellent Very expensive

GREEN MEADOWS PETTING FARM

www.greenmeadowsfarm.com

The low-tech but hands-on Green Meadows is set in natural farmland, complete with a shady, tropical canopy. The two-hour tours allow you to milk a cow, take a donkey ride and get close to the animals.

Off map at F9 1368 South Poinciana Boulevard, Kissimmee 407/846-0770 Daily 9.30–5.30, last tour at 4pm Good Moderate

MUSEUM OF SEMINOLE COUNTY HISTORY

The history of Seminole County (northern Orlando) is brought to life using artifacts donated by the local community.

Off map at c2 300 Bush Boulevard, Sanford 407/665-2489 Tue–Fri 1–5, Sat 9–1 Lynx route 103 Very good Inexpensive

REPTILE WORLD

Find out how to milk a snake at one of the US's biggest snake farms. The snakes have to be "milked" regularly to collect their venom so that it can be used in anti-venom.

Off map at G9 5705 East Irlo Bronson Highway, St. Cloud 407/892-6905 Tue–Sat 9–5, Sun 10–5. Snakes milked at 12 and 3 Good Inexpensive

Waiting to speed through the Everglades on an airboat

Exhibits in the Seminole County Historical Museum

Excursions

THE BASICS

www.buschgardens.com
Off map
10165 North McKinley Drive, Tampa
888/800-5447
Core hours daily 10–6, extended hours throughout the year
Numerous restaurants and cafés
Shuttle bus from Orlando is free with purchase of any Busch Garden ticket. For details of schedules 800/221-1339
Excellent
Very expensive

BUSCH GARDENS

Why include another theme park when, in that department, Orlando is the undisputed champion of the world? Well, because Busch Gardens does what no Orlando park can do; it combines animal attractions, rides, shows and parades to offer what's arguably the perfect combination for the whole family.

The animal attractions, a series of intimate enclosures and vast environments that are part-ride, part-safari park, are first class. Natural landscapes have been meticulously re-created. Watch herds of giraffe, zebra and Thompson's gazelle on the Serengeti Plain; visit the Edge of Africa with its hippos, baboons and meerkats; or ride Rhino Rally. The 2,700 animals make for close encounters by train, jeep or the Skyride, a four-man gondola that glides above the park.

Jungala is based on a jungle theme with exotic animal exhibits, including gibbons and orangutans, and a tiger encounter where you can watch them at play and learn about the work being carried out to save the species worldwide. The tree canopy walk introduces you to jungle vegetation. Book a

Hold on me hearties for a thrilling ride

Hang on in there at the SheiKra splash

Close Up tour, offering behind the scenes animal encounters at each Busch Gardens animal attraction (additional fee).

The rides at Busch Gardens all have great appeal. Orlando has nothing like SheiKra, the US's first dive-coaster, with a 200ft (61m), 45-degree ascent, an Immelmann loop, a 360-degree climbing carousel, a water feature and a top speed of 70mph (112kph). It's a roller-coaster aficionado's dream. SheiKra is complemented by Gwazi, the southeast's largest and fastest double wooden coaster with almost 7,000ft (2,133m) of board. Gwazi incorporates two contrasting sections of track: Gwazi Tiger is designed to give the feeling of riding a bobsled, and Gwazi Lion has continuous spirals. Montu is Busch's inverted coaster; its course subjects your body to a G-force of 3.85. Busch Gardens has plenty of places to get wet. Congo River Rapids is a white-water experience, Tanganyika Tidal Wave ends in a 55ft (16m) watery drop, while Stanley Falls, with its 40ft (12m) drop, is a log-flume ride.

Younger visitors have their own special realm, the Sesame Street Safari of Fun, set in an enchanted forest with a soothing waterfall and a range of rides (height restrictions may apply).

HOW TO GET THERE

Take I-4 west then north on I-75, following signs for Tampa. Exit at 265 on the I-75 (University of South Florida) and take a left off the exit ramp on Fowler Avenue. Turn left at Fowler's intersection with McKinley Drive and follow the road to the park entrance. Total distance 75 miles (120km); time 2 hours.

How scared can you get at Busch Gardens?

THE BASICS

florida.legoland.com
Off map
Legoland Way, off Cypress Gardens Boulevard, Winter Haven. Off US Highway 27, south of Interstate I-4
877/350-5346
Core hours Mon–Fri 10–5, Sat 10–6; later in summer. Closed Tue–Wed Sep to mid-Mar
Restaurants and cafés
Excellent
Expensive
Park shuttle from Orlando daily at 9am from Orlando Premium Outlets—Vineland Ave, inexpensive

TIP

- For a ticket supplement you can combine your visit to LEGOLAND® Florida with a few hours at LEGOLAND® Water Park, with its adrenaline rides and Lazy River.

LEGOLAND® FLORIDA

Enter the world of all things LEGO at Florida's most colorful theme park. There are more than 50 rides and attractions here, all made using the famous LEGO bricks—58 million in total. LEGOLAND® Florida is aimed at kids aged between 2 and12. It's a place where they can let their hair down and have fun, and it's a world where young imaginations can get to work with hands-on experiences found nowhere else in Orlando.

The world's fourth largest toy producer was founded in 1932 by Dane Ole Kirk Kristiansen and is now owned by his grandson. The name LEGO is derived from the Danish phrase "leg godt" meaning "play well."

LEGOLAND® Florida covers 150 acres (60ha) and is split into 11 distinct zones. You can view the whole scene from Island in the Sky, a 100ft (30m) revolving platform, before you head out. Among the highlights is Miniland USA at Fun Town, with scale models of famous American landmarks, including the Kennedy Space Center, the Las Vegas strip and the White House.

Miniland USA

Step back in time at LEGO Kingdoms, inspired by the medieval knights of old. Why not simulate a joust, or jump on The Dragon, a steel roller coaster? Or head to Land of Adventure to ride the Coastersaurus wooden roller coaster, which curves and dips in and around a prehistoric jungle of animated brick dinosaurs, and enter the Lost Kingdom Adventure, an Egyptian-themed ride around a pharaoh's temple.

Kids can try their hand at being a firefighter or cop at LEGO City, where The Ford Driving School also instructs young drivers from ages six through twelve for their first time behind the wheel of their real LEGO automobile. The newest sector of the park is the LEGO World of Chima™. Presented by Cartoon Network, it centers on the company's latest product range and storylines based in a mythical world of animal tribes.

LEGO is about fun, but it also introduces youngsters to engineering and technology through its product ranges. LEGO Technic has the most advanced ride in the park, the LEGO TECHNIC® Coaster, but the Imagination Zone is the most hi-tech sector, with video desks for gaming, and programs for building and controlling LEGO MINDSTORM® robots.

HOW TO GET THERE

Take I-4 west toward Tampa to Exit 55 (US Highway 27 South). Continue south on US Highway 27 and turn right at State Road/Cypress Gardens Boulevard. The park is 4 miles (7km) on the left. Total distance 50 miles (80km); the journey takes about 80 minutes.

DID YOU KNOW?

- 1934 The LEGO name is first used.
- 1964 LEGO bricks make an appearance at the Denmark stand at the World Fair in New York.
- 1973 LEGO USA established.
- 2007 LEGO celebrates its 75th birthday.
- 2011 LEGOLAND® Florida opens.

The Coastersaurus wooden roller coaster

Photo opportunity with a lion

THE BASICS

www.kennedyspacecenter.com
Off map
State Road 405
866/737-5235
9am–dusk; Astronaut Hall of Fame core hours 12–5
Restaurant and café facilities
Excellent
Very expensive

KENNEDY SPACE CENTER

The space race has captured public imagination since the 1960s, and the Kennedy Space Center has been at the heart of the action, launching the Apollo rockets that landed men on the moon and, more recently, the space shuttles. The visitor center is the place to immerse yourself in all things "zero-gravity."

The Kennedy Space Center comprises two separate elements: the Visitor Complex with a range of attractions to explore, and the Space Center itself where certain elements of the vast, working base are accessible on a guided tour. You can also view 10-story-high rockets from all eras of space exploration in the Rocket Garden.

Kennedy Space Center Visitor Complex would make a great attraction even without the working base being here. For budding scientists, it has a fascinating range of experiences to explore, and for more mature visitors it rekindles memories of the earlier space programs.

Where else could you climb into a Space Shuttle without years of astronaut training? Space Shuttle

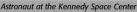

Astronaut at the Kennedy Space Center

Exhibit in the Rocket Garden

Atlantis℠ is the centerpiece of an ongoing 10-year redevelopment of the complex. This $2 billion machine completed 33 shuttle missions and today is the highlight of the attraction, showcasing the 30-year history of the space shuttle program, which ended in 2011. You'll find out just what it feels like to shoot into the atmosphere in a simulated 8-minute shuttle take off, reaching 17,500 mph before you look back on planet Earth, just as the real astronauts did.

HOW TO GET THERE

Take Highway 50 east out of Orlando. At the first traffic light after passing the I-95, turn right on Highway 405 (also Columbia Drive). Follow Highway 405 to the Space Center. Total distance is 50 miles (80km); the journey takes about 80 minutes.

Next door is the Launch Status Center, where you can find out what's happening in real time, or head to the IMAX® theater to feel the exhilaration of walking in space. You'll feel as though you're really out there with the professional crew. Astronauts are on call to answer all your questions. You can have your photograph taken or even have lunch with one.

The serious parts of the tour take you to the NASA compound where launches are planned and executed. You'll visit the LC-39 Observation Gantry, a 60ft (18m) tower with a 360-degree view of the complex, and visit the launch control center and launch pad. Alternatively, you can visit the Apollo/Saturn V Center, which describes the heyday of American space exploration.

All aboard the Space Shuttle

GATORLAND

THE BIG SHOP
www.legoland.com
The ultimate Legoland® emporium with all the ranges for ages 2–12 from first brick sets to themed merchandise, scientific models, apparel and other goodies.
Off map Legoland Florida, One LEGOLAND Way, Winter Haven 877/350-5346

COTTAGE GIFT SHOP
A delightful historic house (*c*1870) with three floors of decorative accessories and collectibles for the home, plus a full range of beauty products and eye-catching jewelry.
Off map 141 West Church Avenue, Longwood 407/834-7220

GATORLAND
www.gatorland.com
Since alligators are no longer a protected species you'll find 'gator skin boots and hats, plus 'gator heads for sale in the gift shop. Also fluffy toys and kitsch items.
K8 14501 South Orange Blossom Trail 800/393-5297 Lynx route 4

GUESS
www.guess.com
Young and vibrant street wear and accessories for men and women.
K4 Florida Mall, 8001 South Orange Blossom Trail 407/888-9880 Lynx routes 4, 7, 37, 42, 107 and 111

KENNEDY SPACE CENTER
The most expensive souvenirs here are the rather cool NASA leather jackets, but there are more affordable items as well: dehydrated astronaut meals, posters, books, DVDs, NASA space games and puzzles, watches and jewelry.
Off map State Road 405, FL 32899 866/737-5235

MEDIEVAL TIMES
www.medievaltimes.com
Some imaginative gifts here, including suits of armor and handmade swords. Kids will love glow-in-the-dark sword and shield sets.
Off map 4510 West Vine Street, Kissimmee 866/543-9637 Lynx routes 55 and 56

A LITTLE EXTRA

If you're flying home, remember to check your luggage allowance with the airline before you start spending. Many bargains are tempting, but with most scheduled airlines limiting check-in baggage to two bags per passenger (max weight for each bag 50lb/23kg) the excess baggage charged could add an unwelcome expense at the end of your trip. The Florida state legislature applies a tax to all sales within its territory and this is currently 6 percent. The amount does not show on the price label—it is added to the purchase price at the register.

NINE WEST
www.ninewest.com
This season's footwear and accessories to accent current fashions.
K4 Florida Mall, 8001 South Orange Blossom Trail 407/859-5455 Lynx routes 4, 7, 37, 42, 107 and 111

OAKLEY
www.oakley.com
Contemporary eyewear, clothing and footwear, so you'll look cool.
K4 Florida Mall, 8001 South Orange Blossom Trail 407/888-6004 Lynx routes 4, 7, 37, 42, 107 and 111

ORLANDO HARLEY-DAVIDSON
www.orlandoharley.com
If you can't afford a motorcyle, try a leather jacket, watch or, if all else fails, a T-shirt of this American classic.
J1 Historic Factory Dealership, 3770 West 37th Street 407/423-0346 Lynx routes 24 and 303

VICTORIA'S SECRET
www.victoriassecret.com
Beautiful women's lingerie, swimwear, nightwear and accessories.
K4 Florida Mall, 8001 South Orange Blossom Trail 407/854-6823 Lynx routes 4, 7, 37, 42, 107 and 111

Entertainment and Nightlife

CAPONE'S DINNER AND SHOW

www.alcapones.com

Step back in time to the 1930s gangland Chicago for a "speakeasy"-style musical revue.

Off map 4740 West Irlo Bronson Highway, Kissimmee 401/397-2378 or 800/220-8428 Shows nightly, times vary Lynx routes 55 and 56

COWBOYS

The premier country nightclub of the region; you can line dance all evening. Live events.

Off map 1108 South Orange Blossom Trail 407/422-7115 Thu–Sat 8pm–2am Lynx routes 4 and 8

MEDIEVAL TIMES

www.medievaltimes.com

Knights on stallions joust to be "King's Champion."

Off map 4510 West Vine Street, Kissimmee 866/543-9637 Nightly—times differ by season Lynx routes 55 and 56

OSCEOLA CENTER FOR THE ARTS

www.ocfta.com

Community arts center hosting exhibitions, theater and local productions.

Off map 2411 East Irlo Bronson Highway, Kissimmee 407/846-6257 Mon–Fri 9–5; evening performances Lynx routes 55 and 56

WAYNE DENSCH PERFORMING ARTS CENTER

Built in the 1920s, the center, which incorporates the Helen Stairs Theater, stages concerts, plays and shows.

Off map 203 South Magnolia Avenue, Sanford 407/321-8111 Ticket office Tue–Sat 10–2 Lynx route 34

Restaurants

PRICES

Prices are approximate, based on a 3-course meal for one person.

$$$	over $60
$$	$30–$60
$	under $30

CRISPERS ($)

www.crispers.com

A great place to stop off for lunch while touring—the menu is packed with fresh salads and stuffed sandwiches.

Off map Colonia Town Park, 1120 Town Park Avenue, Lake Mary 407/833-0901 Lunch, dinner Lynx route 200

DINE WITH AN ASTRONAUT ($$$)

Chat with an astronaut active in today's space program over lunch.

Off map Kennedy Space Center, NASA Parkway, FL 32899 Ticket line 866/737-5235 Lunch

NORMAN'S ($$$)

www.normans.com

Chef Norman van Aken is one of the founding fathers of "New World Cuisine," so come here and feast on the best of his flavors.

J5 Ritz Carlton Hotel, Grande Lakes, 4012 Central Florida Parkway 407/206-2400 Dinner

PRIMO ($$–$$$)

www.primorestaurant.com

Contemporary Italian cuisine featuring organic ingredients from the restaurant's own garden.

J5 Marriott Hotel, Grande Lakes, 4000 Central Florida Parkway 407/393-4444 Dinner Thu–Sun. Closed Jan–Mar

SEASONS 52 ($$)

www.seasons52.com

The seasonally inspired dishes are beautifully cooked and presented.

Off map 463 East Altamonte Drive, Altamonte Springs 407/767-252 Lunch, dinner Lynx route 41

Orlando has over 100,000 hotel rooms and the number is growing all the time. Disney and Universal have invested heavily in their theme resorts and the major American chains are also well represented.

Introduction

Whatever budget you have, you'll find hotel rooms are spacious and always include en-suite facilities. Beds are a generous size and all rooms have multichannel TV and telephone. Balconies and patios are rare in Orlando, especially at the budget end of the spectrum—but then most of the excitement happens away from your hotel.

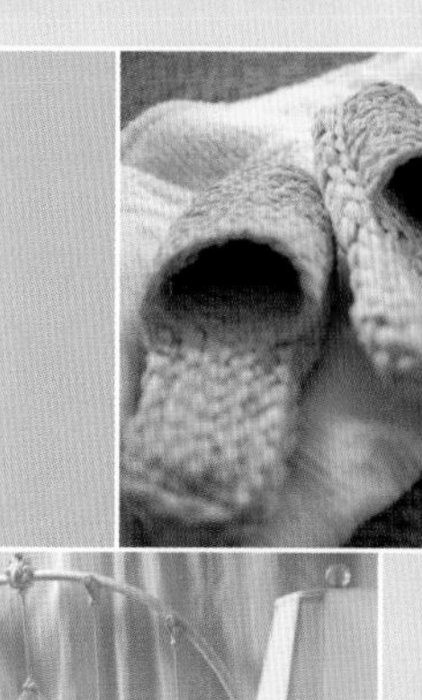

Budget

Orlando's budget hotels tend to be 1970s-motel style with rather dour architecture and rooms entered off external corridors and walkways, or opening directly out onto the parking lot. Most will have a small pool and sun terrace. A new generation of hotels also has small kitchens and a table for at least a little in-room catering.

Mid-range

Mid-range hotels build on the quality and amenities of the budget hotels with better-appointed fittings and more fashionable architecture and styling. Pools are larger, resorts often sit in manicured grounds and there's usually a restaurant on-site.

Expensive

The city's top-class resorts can compete with the best in the world. The architecture and styling is luxurious, amenities are first rate with excellent restaurants, sports, golf and spa facilities. Service is impeccable, and hotels are truly family friendly.

THE FIRST CHOICE

Your main question before you book is... Do you want to stay at the theme parks or away from the theme parks? Disney and Universal hotels offer park perks to their guests, but they are generally more expensive than the independents. Many hotels on International Drive and at Maingate offer free transport to Disney and Universal and dollar-for-dollar they are less expensive, but they may be less convenient if you are planning to spend every day at Disney or Universal.

Budget Hotels

PRICES

Expect to pay up to $150 per night for a budget hotel.

THE COURTYARD AT LAKE LUCERNE

www.orlandohistoricinn.com
This B&B has individually styled rooms along with modern conveniences including kitchenettes and WiFi.
c5 221 Lucerne Circle North East 407/648-5188 Lynx routes 3, 7, 11, 13, 15 and 18

DISNEY ALL-STAR RESORTS

www.disney.go.com
A vast motel-style property with three themes: sports, movies and music. Each of the 5,700 rooms is a self-contained unit. Shuttles to Disney parks.
B8/9 1701 West Buena Vista Drive, Lake Buena Vista 407/939-6000 for hotel or 407/939-1936 for room reservations Lynx routes 303 and 305

EXTENDED STAY AMERICA–CONVENTION CENTER

www.extendedstayamerica.com
Large suites with kitchens right in the heart of the International Drive district. There's a small heated outdoor pool and shuttle to the parks.
G4 8750 Universal Boulevard 407/903-1500, fax 407/903-1555 Lynx routes 8, 38 and 42; I-Ride

FOUR POINTS BY SHERATON ORLANDO STUDIO CITY

www.starwoodhotels.com
This tall tower hotel is a landmark on I-Drive. The 302 rooms have fridges.
H3 5905 International Drive 407/351-2100, fax 407/345-5249 Lynx routes 8, 37, 38 and 42; I-Ride

HAWTHORN SUITES

www.hawthorn.com
Good value one- and two-bedroom studios with kitchens. Pool, plus shuttles to Disney parks.
G5 6435 Westwood Boulevard 407/351-6600 or 800/527-1133, fax 407/351-1977 Lynx route 42; I-Ride

LAKE BUENA VISTA RESORT VILLAGE & SPA

www.lbvorlandoresort.com
Large resort with one-, two-, three- and four-bedroom condo-style units. Large pool with a pirate ship, spa, fitness facilities and a convenience store.
F8 8113 Resort Village Drive, Lake Buena Vista 866/401-2699 or 407/992-0431 Lynx route 304

SAFETY AND SECURITY

- Be security conscious whenever you are around your hotel.
- Don't give your hotel room number to anyone.
- Always verify the identity of anyone who calls at your hotel room.
- If your hotel has a safe deposit box keep all your valuables there.
- Always lock your hotel door on leaving your room.

ROSEN INN AT POINTE ORLANDO

www.roseninn9000.com
Just across the street from Pointe Orlando (▷ 63) and within walking distance of many I-Drive attractions, this is a great location for couples and families. Small pool, plus WiFi and flat-screen TVs in rooms.
G4 9000 International Drive 407/996-8585 or 800/999-8585 Lynx routes 8, 38, 42, 58 and 111; I-Ride

ROYALE PARC SUITES

www.royaleparcsuitesorlando.com
Family hotel with one- and two-bedroom suites. Buffet breakfast is included in the rate. In walking distance of Old Town; shuttles to main parks.
E9 5876 West Irlo Bronson Highway, Kissimmee 407/396-8040, fax 407/396-6766 Lynx routes 55 and 56

SERALAGO HOTEL AND SUITES

www.seralagohotel.com
Family-friendly resort with pools, playgrounds and tennis. Kids' Suites with kitchen allow families to sleep in one unit. All 614 rooms have a fridge. Shuttle to Disney parks.
D9 5678 Irlo Bronson Highway, Kissimmee 407/396-4488, fax 407/396-8915 Lynx routes 55 and 56

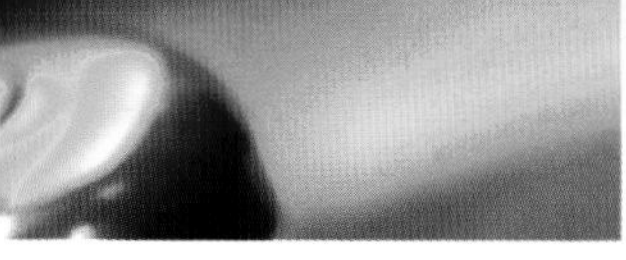

Mid-Range Hotels

PRICES

Expect to pay between $150 and $250 per night for a mid-range hotel.

BOHEMIAN HOTEL CELEBRATION

www.celebrationhotel.com

This clapboard boutique hotel, with 115 rooms, sits on the lakeside at Celebration with shopping and dining close by. Shuttles to Disney parks.
D9 700 Bloom Street 407/556-6000 or 888/249-4007, fax 407/566-1844

CARIBE ROYALE

www.cariberoyale.com

This huge pink resort is set in 45 acres (18ha) and has a conference center. With 1,218 one-bedroom suites and 120 two-bedroom villas, it has ample capacity. Amenities include the Venetian Room restaurant and a fantastic free-form swimming pool.
F8 8101 World Center Drive 800/823-8300 or 407/238-8000 Lynx route 304

CASTLE HOTEL

www.marriott.com

This is one of the most interesting hotels on International Drive. The luxurious rooms are less dramatic but are still plush and comfortable.
G4 8629 International Drive 407/345-1511, fax 407/248-8181 Lynx routes 8, 38, 42, 58 and 111; I-Ride

CROWNE PLAZA UNIVERSAL

www.cporlando.com

One block from I-Drive, the Crowne Plaza is both a tourist and a business hotel, with pool, fitness room and laundry. There is a shuttle service to Disney and Universal.
G3 7800 Universal Boulevard 407/355-0550, 866/864-8627 for reservations, fax 407/355-0504 Lynx route 21; I-Ride

DISNEY'S CORONADO SPRINGS RESORT

www.disney.go.com

The Coronado's 1,900 guest rooms are set around a natural lake. The food court offers a range of dining for families.
B8 1000 West Buena Vista Drive, Lake Buena Vista 407/939-7675 for vacation package bookings, 407/939-1000 hotel direct line or 407/939-1936 for room only bookings, fax 407/939-1001 Lynx routes 303 and 305

HERITAGE PROPERTIES

Although the hotels of Orlando and the park areas are predominantly modern build properties, you can find places to stay that hark back to times gone by. Two hotels date from the 1920s, Park Plaza Hotel (▷ 111) in Winter Park and Eô Inn (▷ this page) downtown. The Courtyard at Lake Lucerne (▷ 109), also downtown, has rooms in four mansions, all dating from the start of the 20th century.

DISNEY'S PORT ORLEANS RESORT

www.disney.go.com

The resort takes its theme from French Quarter architecture and styling in downtown New Orleans, with formal gardens and a lakeside setting. Cozy rooms with wooden furniture and southern-theme eateries on-site
D7 2201 Orleans Drive, Lake Buena Vista 407/939-7675 for vacation package bookings, 407/934-5000 hotel direct line or 407/939-1936 for room only bookings Lynx route 300

EMBASSY SUITES JAMAICA COURT

www.embassysuites.com

At the lower end of the medium price range, this International Drive Hotel has comfortable guest rooms decorated in tropical colors. Indoor, as well as an outdoor pool.
G4 8250 Jamaican Court, International Drive 407/345-8250 or 800/560-7782 in US, 800 44 45 86 67 in UK, fax 407/ 352-1463 Lynx routes 8, 38 and 42; I-Ride

EÕ INN & SPA

www.eoinn.com

This interesting 1923 mansion in the heart of Thornton Park has been tastefully renovated into a 17-room boutique hotel and spa with luxurious modern fittings and relax-

ing neutral hues. Rooftop terrace with hot tub.
c4 227 North Eola Drive, Thornton Park 407/481-8485 or 888/481-8488, fax 407/481-8495 Lynx routes 85, 6 and 15

FLORIDAYS RESORT ORLANDO
www.floridaysresortorlando.com
This bright condo-resort offers spacious two- and three-bedroomed units with full kitchens. Pool and gym plus all-day eatery and shop on site.
G6 12562 International Drive 407/238-7700 Lynx routes 8, 38 and 42; I-Ride

HYATT PLACE ORLANDO/ CONVENTION CENTER
www.hyatt.com
A 2008 full-service hotel from this prestigious chain has 42-inch flat screen and corner sitting area in each room. Small outdoor pool, gym and café. Breakfast included.
G4 8741 International Drive 407/370-4720, fax 407/370-4721 Lynx routes 8, 38 and 42; I-Ride

J. W. MARRIOT
www.grandelakes.com
Sharing the magnificent Grande Lakes site with the Ritz Carlton, this hotel offers exceptional golf and a fantastic spa on-site, along with a range of upscale eating opportunities. Rooms are plush and well furnished.
J5 4040 Central Florida Parkway 407/206-2300 or 888/236-2427, fax 407/206-2301

MARRIOTT ORLANDO LAKE MARY
www.marriott.com
A well-appointed hotel that makes a good base for exploring Seminole County. It's close to Wekiwa and to the zoo. There is a range of restaurants in the new malls within walking distance, plus the hotel's own eateries.
Off map 135 International Parkway, Lake Mary 407/995-1100 or 800/380-7724, fax 407/995-1150 Lynx route 200

NICKELODEON FAMILY SUITES
www.nickhotel.com
Aimed very much at the family market, the Nick accommodations are spacious and colorful and there's a lot to do within the resort, including a kids' spa, live theater complex, games arcade and two activity pools. The on-site laundry might also be useful.
E8 14500 Continental Gateway 407/387-5437 or 877/642-5111, fax 407/387-1489 Lynx route 304

PARENTS' NIGHT OFF

Nickelodeon Family Suites offer a special fully supervised evening program for children ages 5 to 12 called Nick After Dark. It includes interactive science demonstrations, games and entertainment, plus a choice of meals. This means parents can enjoy a meal, show or movie knowing that their kids are also enjoying their evening in a safe environment. Reserve at least 24 hours in advance.

PARK PLAZA HOTEL
www.parkplazahotel.com
This hotel harks back to an earlier era and rooms are individually furnished.
D2 307 Park Avenue South, Winter Park 407/647-1072, fax 407/647-4081 Lynx routes 102 and 443

STAYBRIDGE SUITES
www.ichotels.com
Well placed for the Disney parks and the restaurants and shopping of Lake Buena Vista, the Staybridge offers the comfort of an apartment (with equipped kitchen) and the amenities of a small hotel. Outdoor pool and fitness center.
E6 Suiteside Drive, Lake Buena Vista 407/238-0777 Lynx route 300

WESTIN GRAND BOHEMIAN
www.grandbohemianhotel.com
From this luxurious downtown hotel you can reach the city's best bars on foot. Rooftop pool.
C4 325 South Orange Avenue 407/313-9000 or 866/663-0024, fax 407/313-9001 Lynx routes 3, 6, 7, 11, 13, 18 and 51; Lymmo

Luxury Hotels

Expect to pay more than $250 per night for a luxury hotel.

DISNEY'S GRAND FLORIDIAN SPA RESORT
www.disney.go.com
The flagship of Disney's portfolio, the Grand Floridian has sandy beaches on the Seven Seas Lagoon. There are restaurants and a spa
B5 4401 Grand Floridian Drive 407/938-7675 for vacation package bookings, 407/824-3000 hotel direct line or 407/939-1936 for room only bookings Lynx route 302

DISNEY'S YACHT AND BEACH CLUB RESORT
www.disney.go.com
The lakeside clubs are inspired by the seaside villages of America's northeast.
C7 1700–1800 Epcot Resort Boulevard 407/938-7675 for vacation package bookings, 407/934-8000 hotel direct line or 407/939-1936 for room only bookings Lynx route 303

HYATT REGENCY-GRAND CYPRESS
www.hyatt.com
A grand hotel anchored by a Jack Nicklaus-designed golf course. Pool, restaurants and spa.
E6 1 Grand Cypress Boulevard, off route 535 407/239-1234, fax 407/239-3800

MARRIOTT IMPERIAL PALM VILLAS
www.marriott.com
The 46 one- or two-bedroom apartments make it a cozy place to stay.
F7 8404 Vacation Way 407/238-6200, fax 407/238-6247 Lynx route 300

PORTOFINO BAY
www.loewshotels.com
Styled as a Mediterranean seaside village, there are waterside walkways and themed restaurants here. It's within walking distance of Universal parks, with free transport to SeaWorld, Discovery Cove and Wet 'n Wild.
G2 5601 Universal Boulevard 888/430-4999 for bookings, fax 407/503-1010

RENAISSANCE ORLANDO SEAWORLD RESORT
www.marriott.com
The Olympic-size pool is a feature of this huge hotel, which has a golf course. The 778 rooms are well furnished. Those at the front have good views of the nightly SeaWorld fireworks.
G5 6677 Sea Harbor Drive 407/351-5555 or 800/327-6677, fax 407/351-9991 Lynx routes 8 and 50; I-Ride

THE MAGICARD

The Orlando MagiCard gives a range of visitor benefits, including discounts on many attractions. The major cost saving comes in the accommodations section, with hotels in various price ranges offering discounts to card members. Book this before arriving in Orlando by downloading the MagiCard from the Convention and Visitors Bureau website at www.visitorlando.com.

RITZ CARLTON GRANDE LAKES
www.grandelakes.com
The Ritz Carlton offers 584 luxurious rooms, a spa and a highly regarded golf course.
J5 4012 Central Florida Parkway 407/206-2400 or 800/628-3665, fax 407/206-2401

ROSEN SHINGLE CREEK
www.rosenshinglecreek.com
This 1,500-room and suite resort has an 18-hole golf course, a choice of dining and a spa. Rooms have a high standard of amenities.
J$ 9939 Universal Boulevard 407/996-6338 or 866/996-6338, fax 407/996-9938 Lynx route 58

ROYAL PACIFIC RESORT UNIVERSAL ORLANDO
www.loewshotels.com
This sophisticated resort takes its design influences from the South Seas. Rooms feature tropical wood and bamboo with imported Asian art. Good range of amenities.
J5 6300 Hollywood Way 407/503-3000 or 888/430-4999 for bookings, fax 407/503-3010

Practical information for your trip, covering when to go, how to get there and how to get around once you've arrived, plus useful websites for planning your itinerary and what to do in an emergency.

Planning Ahead

When to Go

Orlando's attractions stay open throughout the year. For the best weather, visit during October and November, March and April, when the weather is warm but the air is not too humid. The quietest times at the theme parks are September until Thanksgiving (third Thursday in November). The busiest times are around the major holidays and June to August.

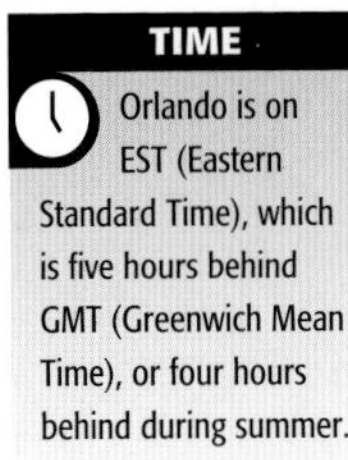

TIME

Orlando is on EST (Eastern Standard Time), which is five hours behind GMT (Greenwich Mean Time), or four hours behind during summer.

AVERAGE DAILY MAXIMUM TEMPERATURES

JAN	FEB	MAR	APR	MAY	JUN	JUL	AUG	SEP	OCT	NOV	DEC
72°F	73°F	77°F	81°F	81°F	86°F	90°F	90°F	86°F	82°F	77°F	72°F
22°C	23°C	25°C	27°C	27°C	30°C	32°C	32°C	30°C	28°C	25°C	22°C

Spring has warm days. Rain and short storms are possible at any time, all year round.
Summer (Jun–Sep) is extremely hot and humid with regular thunderstorms. This is also hurricane season. Direct hits from big storms are rare, but the area suffered three in 2004.
Fall offers cooler temperatures and quieter weather. Nights are still warm.
Winter has average daytime temperatures in the low 70s Fahrenheit (early 20s Celsius), though be aware that temperatures may drop much further. Pack a sweater!

WHAT'S ON

January *The Capitol One Bowl*, classic New Year's Day football match at Orlando's Capitol One Bowl Stadium.
February *Silver Spurs Rodeo* in Kissimmee is the biggest cowboy gathering in Florida, with a full program of bull and bronco riding contests.
Arts Festival sees the Bach Festival Society host concerts at Rollins College, Winter Park.
Four weekends leading up to *Mardi Gras* (and the nights themselves) turn Universal CityWalk® into party central.
March The *Arnold Palmer Invitational Golf Tournament* at the Bay Hill Club is hosted by Arnold Palmer.
Watch *baseball spring training* with the Atlanta Braves at Disney's Wild World of Sport and the Houston Astros at Osceola Heritage Park, Kissimmee.
Winter Park Sidewalk Arts Festival sees national and international artists displaying their works.
Late March/early April *Florida Film Festival*.
May *Orlando International Fringe Festival*: 10 days of irreverent comedy performances.
October See *Silver Spurs Rodeo* (part 2) at Kissimmee.
Halloween: the weekend leading up to the event turns CityWalk into a partying "ghoul town."
The International Food Festival at Epcot® runs into early November.
November The *Festival of the Masters* is an arts festival at Downtown Disney West Side.
December Disney's Magic Kingdom® is turned into a *Christmas* wonderland with an impressive array of festive decorations, concerts, parades and fireworks displays.

Useful Websites

The Internet is a goldmine of information about Orlando. You can check what is going on at the theme parks and make bookings online.

www.visitorlando.com
The official website of the Orlando Convention and Visitors Bureau with information on what to do and where to go. Links to websites to book discounted accommodations. You can also order booklets and buy the MagiCard.

experiencekissimmee.com
Kissimmee's official website with information on attractions in the downtown area and along I-192 (Irlo Bronson Memorial Highway). Book discount hotels through the site.

www.visitseminole.com
Official Seminole County Convention and Visitors Bureau, with information on attractions in Orlando's most natural region, plus "what's on" and hotel information.

www.disneyworld.disney.go.com
Disney's official website with information on all parks and resorts. You can book accommodations and restaurant tables.

allears.net
An easy-to-navigate unofficial Disney site that has lots of practical tips and background on enjoying Walt Disney World® Resort.

www.universalorlando.com
Universal Orlando's official site. A good overview, with the ability to book hotel rooms and restaurants. Useful to find out what's happening at Universal CityWalk®.

www.nps.gov
Official website of the American National Park Service with details on how to visit all the parks and background information on their animals, birds and natural environments.

PRIME TRAVEL SITE

www.fodors.com
A travel-planning site where you can research prices and weather, book tickets, vehicles and rooms, and ask questions; links to other sites.

BOOKING AHEAD

With thousands of people visiting the major parks every day, popular restaurants/shows sell out quickly, so it makes sense to book ahead.

Disney
The Walt Disney World® Resort website disneyworld.disney.go.com is a one-stop location for booking park tickets, resort hotels, shows and restaurants. The important telephone numbers (7am–11pm Eastern Time) are 407/939-5277 (general information); 407/939-1936 (hotel reservations); 407/939-1947 (restaurant reservations); 407/939-7679 (tickets and special events).

Universal Orlando
The Universal website www.universalorlando.com allows you to book tickets and hotel rooms ahead. The important telephone numbers (8.30am–7pm Eastern Time) are 407/224-7840 (buying tickets); 877/801-9720 (vacation packages); 407/224-4233 (guest services).

Getting There

ENTRY REQUIREMENTS

All foreign visitors entering the US require a valid passport. Canadians can also enter the US across land or sea borders with a NEXUS card. Citizens of Australia, Germany, Ireland, New Zealand and the UK (plus most other EU countries) can arrive in the US for less than 90 days for business or pleasure under the Visa Waiver Scheme provided that they have a machine-readable passport with at least six months' validity on it. They must also complete an Electronic System of Travel Authorization (ESTA) before they travel to the US. ESTA is a web-based system and can only be accessed online. For more information, and to complete the ESTA, visit esta.cbp.dhs.gov. Others should consult the American Embassy in their own country for the latest visa requirements. Regulations can change so always check before you travel.

AIRPORTS

There are direct flights from continental Europe to Orlando's international airport, but most transatlantic flights are routed via London. Airport facilities include an information desk, a small number of shops (including a pharmacy), bureaux de change, restaurants and car rental.

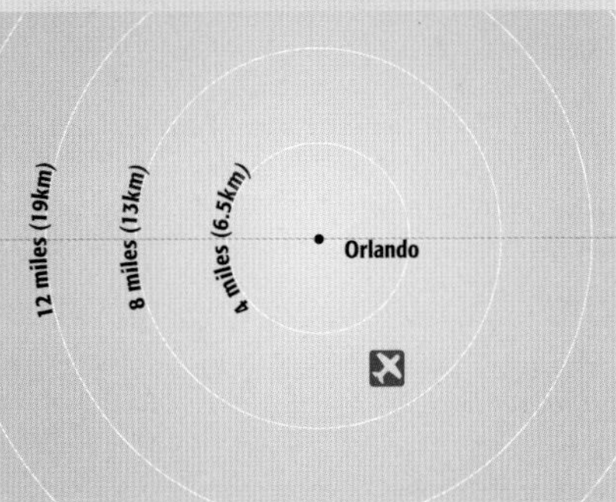

FROM ORLANDO INTERNATIONAL AIRPORT

The primary international airport is Orlando International (MCO) ☎ 407/825-2001, flight info 407/825-8463; www.orlandoairports.net, 6.5 miles (10.5km) southeast of the city. The downtown journey takes about 20 minutes, International Drive takes 30 minutes and Walt Disney World® Resort 45 minutes. Lynx public bus services are 11 and 51 to downtown, 41 to Apopka and 42 to International Drive. Route 111 links the airport with the Disney University via Magic Kingdom® park transport hub. An airport shuttle can be booked to most hotels in the tourist areas. Mears (☎ 407/432-5566; www. mearsstransportation.com) is the major supplier. Prices one-way: International Drive $20–$30; Disney area $26–$36; downtown $28–$36.

Walt Disney World® Resort operates a free shuttle, Disney's Magical Express, from Orlando International Airport to all Disney® Resort Hotels Orlando, except the Walt Disney World Swan and Dolphin hotel and the Downtown Disney Resort area hotels. You will travel directly to your hotel

and they will collect all bags at the airport and deliver them to your room. This service is available only to Walt Disney World® Resort guests. If you're not staying at a Disney hotel, take a taxi from the airport. Daytime fares per cab are about $35 to Universal Studios and International Drive, $55 to Epcot® (slightly more to the Magic Kingdom® area) and $35 to the downtown area. Reliable companies include Yellow/City Cab (☎ 407/422-2222; www.mearstransportation.com), Diamond Cab Company (407/523-3333; www.diamondcabco.com) and Transtar (407/888-5530; www.mytranstar.com).

FROM SANFORD INTERNATIONAL AIRPORT

The secondary airport for the city is Sanford International (SFB), 18 miles (11km) northwest of the downtown area (☎ 407/585-4000; www.orlandosanfordairport.com). There are flights to smaller American cities and Sanford accommodates charter flights from the UK and Western Europe. Journey time to the downtown area is 45 minutes. It is an hour to International Drive and at least 1 hour 15 minutes to the Disney area. The taxi service from the airport (☎ 407/422-2222) has prices to downtown from about $70, to International Drive from $90 and to Walt Disney World® Resort from $115.

BY BUS

Greyhound services link Orlando with the rest of the US. There are stations at Downtown (✉ 555 John Young Parkway ☎ 407/292-3424) and Kissimmee (✉ 103 East Dakin Avenue ☎ 407/ 847-3911). For information on routes and costs consult www.greyhound.com.

BY RAIL

The vast Amtrak passenger network has stations in downtown Orlando (✉ 1400 Sligh Boulevard), Winter Park (✉ 150 West Morse Boulevard) and Kissimmee (✉ 111 Dakin Street). Customer service can be contacted on ☎ 800/872-7245; www.amtrak.com.

INSURANCE

It is vital to have comprehensive medical insurance as all treatment is chargeable and costs can be high. It is also advisable to have insurance for loss or theft of your property and documents, and to cover any travel delays or cancellations. Numerous insurance companies sell combined insurance packages for either a single trip or on an annual multitrip basis.

AIRPORT SECURITY

- Passengers are currently asked to limit carry-on liquids to 3oz (100ml) bottles or less, which must be presented at security check points in a 1qt (1l) clear plastic bag; one bag per passenger.
- All footwear and coats must be removed for X-ray.
- All checked-in baggage will be X-rayed in the US and hand-checked if necessary, so don't lock cases.
- Arrive at the airport in good time.
- Contact your airline before travel to check for any new security arrangements.

Getting Around

VISITORS WITH DISABILITIES

Facilities for visitors with disabilities are generally excellent in Orlando, with toilet facilities, ramps and automatic doors or special entrances in all public buildings, shopping malls and tourist attractions. Most public walkways feature ramps at street intersections. All public transport buses have wheelchair access. Most hotels have some rooms specifically designed for disabled guests. The majority of organizations have TTY (Text Telephone) services for the deaf or hard of hearing and many have Braille information for visitors with visual impairment.

FREE SHUTTLE BUSES

If you don't want to rent a car, then a stay on International Drive will mean (usually) free shuttle bus access to the major parks (30 minutes to Disney, 15 minutes to Universal) and I-Ride for the attractions along the Drive itself. If you stay at a Disney or Universal hotel and only intend to visit the resort parks, complimentary transport will be available.

BUSES

Orlando has a good public bus system, Lynx, but the distances involved can mean long journey times and the timetables to Walt Disney World® Resorts make it impractical for tourist use. The system runs daily 4.30am–12.15am, with reduced services on holidays. Buses must be accessed from a Lynx bus stop; look for a round emblem of a lynx footprint. Signs correspond to the color of the particular route or "link." The transport authority also runs Lymmo, a free circular bus service that links downtown areas with the Lynx Central Station (☒ 455 North Garland Avenue ☎ 407/841-5969, www.golynx.com) and venues near the Bob Carr Center. It runs every 5 minutes during office hours, 10–15 minutes at other times. The I-Ride trolleybus (☎ 866/243-7483; www.iridetrolley.com) has two routes linking the attractions along International Drive. It operates 8am–10.30pm every day and can be accessed from the numbered stops that are positioned along its routes.

WHERE TO GET MAPS

- Lynx: get route maps from all terminus offices or the Orlando/Orange County Convention and Visitors Bureau office at ☒ 8723 International Drive.
- I-Ride: from the Orlando/Orange County Convention and Visitors Bureau and hotels where passes are sold.

DISCOUNTS/TYPES OF TICKETS

- Lynx: tickets cost $2 and are valid for 90 minutes from first use.
- Day passes (valid from 4am on the day of use to 3am the following morning) cost $4.50, and a 7-day pass is $16.
- Senior citizens, under 18s and disabled travelers benefit from reduced fares.
- Single fare and day passes are available on the bus (cash only, no change given). Other passes are available at Lynx offices, and some supermarkets and shops (see website or Lynx route map).
- I-Ride: single fares are $2, senior citizens pay

$0.25 and child (3–9) $1. No change offered.
● Day passes cost $5 per person, 3-day passes $7, 5-day passes $9, 7-day passes $12 and 14-day passes $18. Passes are sold at the Tourist Office and at hotels and shops.

TAXIS

Official taxis are painted yellow with the word TAXI on the sides and a lighted sign on the roof. Taxi stands can be found outside all attractions, major hotels and airport arrival terminals. All hotels and most restaurants will be happy to call a taxi for you. Taxis will have a meter and rates will be posted inside. Make sure that the meter is set correctly for the location and the time of day. Never use an unofficial taxi. Taxi fares from the station to International Drive cost $30 and to the Disney area $48.

CAR RENTAL

Orlando is not compact and to make the most of what the city has to offer, you need to rent a car. It's 15 miles (24km) south from downtown to the Disney parks or to Kissimmee and 10 miles (16km) to International Drive. Head north and it's 3 miles (5km) to Winter Park, 12 miles (20km) to Wekiwa Springs and 20 miles (32km) to the Central Florida Zoo. Car rental rates are competitive. It is best to take an unlimited mileage deal; check it includes collision damage waiver and that you have more than adequate insurance. The minimum age is often 21 (sometimes 25), and there is a surcharge on drivers under 25. You will most likely be asked to pay by credit card. Try these established companies:
Alamo ☎ 888/233-8745; Avis ☎ 800/633-3469; Budget ☎ 800/218-7992; Dollar ☎ 800/800-4000; Enterprise ☎ 800/261-7331; Hertz ☎ 800/654-3131; National ☎ 877/222-9058; Thrifty ☎ 800/847-4389.
Remember that Florida state law demands that all children under five must travel in a federally approved child restraint (safety seat, booster seat or belt) in the back seat of the vehicle. These will incur an extra cost.

ORGANIZED TOURS

Orlando is not a destination that is conducive to organized tours. When so many of its attractions require at least half a day, or a full day for the major theme parks, the itineraries would be impossible. However, some theme parks offer tailor-made tours as an extra package. SeaWorld has a six-hour park tour with a guide and front-of-line access, guaranteed show seating and animal encounters. It also offers one-hour, behind-the-scenes tours for $29 (C888/800-5447; www.seaworld.com).
Walt Disney World® Resort has several behind-the-scenes tours, but none has guided tours of the rides and shows. The full-day Backstage Magic explores behind the scenes at Epcot®, Disney's Hollywood Studios and Disney's Magic Kingdom® for $249. Others include the three-hour Gardens of the World at Epcot® ($60) or the five-hour behind-the-scenes Keys to the Kingdom tour of Magic Kingdom® ($79).
Universal Studios offers the VIP Experience, an escorted tour with line-skipping and back-stage access. A 1-day 1 park experience is $170
The Orlando Museum of Art will provide guided tours for 10 people or more with 10 days' notice (Tue–Fri, $9 per person).

Essential Facts

MONEY

The unit of currency is the dollar (= 100 cents). Bills (notes) come in denominations of \$1, \$5, \$10, \$20, \$50 and \$100; coins come in 25¢ (a quarter), 10¢ (a dime), 5¢ (a nickel) and 1¢ (a penny). The best place to exchange non-US currency is at a bank. US dollar traveler's checks are the most secure way to carry money and they are accepted as cash in most places. US dollars can be obtained from Automatic Teller Machines (ATMs) with either credit or debit cards if you have a Personal Identification Number (PIN). ATMs are plentiful. Some charge an extra fee for their use. Credit cards are universally accepted. Automatic payment machines, such as in gas stations, may not accept foreign cards.

ELECTRICITY

- Power supply is 110/120 volts AC (60 cycles).
- A transformer is needed for 240-volt electrical equipment.

EMBASSIES AND CONSULATES

- British Consul ✉ 1001 Brickell Bay Drive, Miami ☎ 305/400-6400.
- British Embassy ✉ 3100 Massachusetts Avenue North West, Washington D.C. ☎ 202/588-6500.
- German Embassy ✉ 2300 M Street NW, Washington DC ☎ 202/298-4000.
- Canadian Embassy ✉ 501 Pennsylvania Avenue North West, Washington DC ☎ 202/682-1740.
- Eire ✉ 2234 Massachusetts Avenue North West, Washington DC ☎ 202/462-3939.
- Australia ✉ 1601 Massachusetts Avenue North West, Washington DC ☎ 202/797-3000.
- New Zealand ✉ 37 Observatory Circle North West, Washington DC ☎ 202/328-4800.

EMERGENCIES

- Dial 911 to access all the emergency services. Explain your circumstances and location to the operator and the appropriate service will be rapidly dispatched.

LONE AND WOMEN TRAVELERS

- Most hotels don't charge a single person occupancy supplement.
- There is little fear of being hassled.
- Bear in mind the advice given under sensible precautions (▷ 122).

LOST PROPERTY

- Check with the front desk at your hotel.
- Public transport, taxi firms and all tourist attractions will have a lost property department.
- Report all stolen or lost credit cards to the police immediately.
- You will need a police report to make an insurance claim on your return home.

MAILING A LETTER/POSTCARD

- Post offices: US post offices are usually open Mon–Fri 9–5, but are not always in obvious locations. International Drive has post offices at ✉ 8723 International Drive and Mall at Millennia.
- Vending machines sell stamps but at a 25 percent premium.
- Hotels and most major attractions often provide postal services.

MEDICAL TREATMENT

- There are charges for all medical treatment in the US. It is therefore imperative that visitors have insurance that covers any medical problems. Look for policies with a minimum $5,000,000 limit.
- The quality of facilities and staff expertise are extremely high.
- Full service hospital ✉ 601 East Rollins Street ☎ 407/303-5600.
- Walk-in medical centers at ✉ 12500 S. Apopka Vineland Road ☎ 407/934-2273 (close to Downtown Disney®) and ✉ 8014 Conroy Windermere Road ☎ 407/291-9960 (close to the Universal Studios®).
- All major attractions will have good first-aid stations to help with both major and minor incidents. Ask a member of staff for immediate help.
- Pharmacies stock a wide range of medicines available without prescription.
- Pharmacies must employ a qualified pharmacist who can advise on a range of minor ailments and suggest suitable treatments.

NATIONAL HOLIDAYS

- Jan 1: New Year's Day; 3rd Mon Jan: Martin Luther King Day; 3rd Mon Feb: Presidents' Day; Mar/Apr: Easter; Last Mon May: Memorial Day; Jul 4: Independence Day; 1st Mon Sep: Labor Day; 2nd Mon Oct: Columbus Day; Nov 11: Veterans' Day; 4th Thu Nov: Thanksgiving; Dec 25: Christmas Day; Boxing Day (Dec 26) is not a public holiday in the US. Some stores open on national holidays.

TOURIST OFFICES

✉ 8723 International Drive, Orlando ☎ 407/363-5872 🕒 Daily 8.30–6.30.
✉ 4155 West Vine Street, Kissimmee ☎ 407/742-8200 🕒 Daily 9–5.
✉ 151 West Lyman Avenue, Winter Park ☎ 407/664-8281 🕒 Mon–Fri 8.30–5, Sat 9–2.

NEWSPAPERS/ MAGAZINES

- The *Orlando Sentinel* is the main local daily with national news and international headlines.
- *USA Today* is the most widely read daily national. It is available at hotel reception desks and from self-service vending machines.
- English and other European newspapers can be bought at Street Corner News ✉ Florida Mall

STUDENT TRAVELERS

Most hotel rooms sleep four (in two queen beds), so rates work well for groups of travelers. There is one hostel in Orlando, Palm Lakefront Resort and Hostel (✉ 4840 West Irlo Bronson Highway (Highway 192), Kissimmee ☎ 407/396-1759; www.orlandohostels.com). Some museums offer discounts for student visitors.

RADIO/TELEVISION

There are numerous commercial television stations and most hotels offer 20–30 channels. Local stations providing programming and news are WESH and FOX 35. Radio is a commercialized arena, so simply tune to the music/talk station you like.

TELEPHONES

Most hotels have international and local dialing. Local calls will be free or cheap; long-distance and international calls attract a premium. For these use a low-cost provider such as AT&T who will issue you an access number. Prepaid phone cards are sold at drugstores and visitor centers. Calls are charged at a fixed rate. If traveling with your own phone from outside the US, T-Mobile and AT&T offer inexpensive packages to call/text home. Public telephones are plentiful. These operate with cash, credit cards or calling cards and can be used for long-distance and international calls. From public phones dial 0 for the operator; dial 1 plus the area code for numbers within the US and Canada; dial 411 to find US and Canadian numbers.

- International dialing codes: Dial 011 followed by
UK: 44
Ireland: 353
Australia: 61

OPENING HOURS

- Stores: most independent stores open Mon–Sat 9–5.30 or 9–7.
- Malls: usually open Mon–Sat 10–9 and Sun 12–6.
- Banks: larger branches may have a drive-through service on Sat 8–noon.
- Post offices: Mon–Fri 9–5, some open longer weekdays and Sat 9–noon.
- Museums: hours vary but core hours are 10–5.
- Theme parks: theme park hours vary seasonally and daily. Core winter hours are10–5; core summer hours 9–8.

SENSIBLE PRECAUTIONS

- High temperatures can cause dehydration. Keep fluid levels up and avoid too much coffee and alcohol.
- The Florida sun is very strong. Wear a hat, cover arms and legs and use a strong sunscreen.
- Feet are prone to blisters during long days at parks. Wear comfortable shoes and carry Band-Aids to cover pressure points.
- Mosquitoes can be a nuisance at places such as National Parks. Apply a good repellent and keep arms covered.
- Ticks can carry disease. During summer months check for bites after you've walked or hiked in the backwoods and see a doctor if you find evidence of bites. Don't attempt to remove a tick yourself.
- Make a copy of your travel tickets, itinerary and important items such as your passport number and credit card numbers. Keep these separate from your genuine documents.
- Beware of carrying expensive items such as jewelry or cameras.
- Don't carry large amounts of cash.
- Don't leave anything of value in your car and make sure nothing is on show when you park it.
- At night, drive on well-lit streets. Walk in well-lit busy streets.
- If in doubt, take taxis rather than walking into unfamiliar territory.

Language

The official language of the US is English and, given that one-third of all overseas visitors come from the UK, Orlando natives have few problems coping with British accents and dialects. Spanish is also widely spoken, as many workers in the hotel and catering industries are of Latin origin. Many English words have different meanings and below are some words in common usage where they differ from the English spoken in the UK:

USEFUL WORDS	
shop	*store*
chemist (shop)	*drugstore*
cinema	*movie theater*
film	*movie*
pavement	*sidewalk*
toilet	*restroom*
trousers	*pants*
nappy	*diaper*
glasses	*eyeglasses*
policeman	*cop*
post	*mail*
surname	*last name*
holiday	*vacation*
handbag	*purse*
cheque	*check*
banknote	*bill*
cashpoint	*automatic teller*
autumn	*fall*

ACCOMMODATIONS	
ground floor	*first floor*
first floor	*second floor*
flat	*apartment*
lift	*elevator*
eiderdown	*comforter*
tap	*faucet*
luggage	*baggage*
suitcase	*trunk*
hotel porter	*bellhop*
chambermaid	*room maid*
cupboard	*closet*

FOOD	
grilled	*broiled*
prawns	*shrimp*
aubergine	*eggplant*
courgette	*zucchini*
chips	*fries*
crisps	*chips*
biscuit	*cookie*
scone	*biscuit*
sorbet	*sherbet*
jelly	*jello*
jam	*jelly*
sweets	*candy*
spirit	*liquor*
soft drink	*soda*

TRAVEL	
car	*automobile*
bonnet	*hood*
boot	*trunk*
repair	*fix*
caravan	*trailer*
lorry	*truck*
motorway	*freeway*
main road	*highway*
petrol	*gas*
railway	*railroad*
tram	*streetcar*
platform	*track*
buffer	*bumper*
car park	*parking lot*

Timeline

THE SENATOR AND THE PHOENIX

The oldest cypress tree in the United States used to be in Orlando. Estimated to be around 3,500 years old, the 136ft (41.5m) high sentinel, named The Senator, was a sapling during the age of the Egyptian pharaohs. Tragedy struck in January 2012 when The Senator was destroyed in an arson attack and Florida residents mourned its loss. But The Senator wasn't completely lost. In the late 1990s a local science team had taken a graft from a branch that had fallen from The Senator in a storm. Seven of these grafts had grown into fine young trees—clones of the original. In March 2013 a 50ft (15m) clone named Phoenix was planted beside the old tree. Floridians hope that it will carry the fine tradition at Big Tree Park on for another 3,500 years.

From left: Seminole bronze statue; Rocket Garden at Kennedy Space Center; Universal Studios®; Seminole dolls for sale; orange tree

c10,000BC The first humans settle in the St. John's River area of Central Florida.

c500BC Timucuan (▷ 79) tribes arrive.

1513 Europeans, in the form of the Spanish, bring cattle, and diseases that wipe out the Timucuan.

1500–1700s Central Florida remains mainly untouched by European settlement.

Late 1700s Native American Seminoles, pushed south by European colonization, settle in the area. At the same time settlers descended from Scottish and Irish immigrants and known as "Crackers" move inland.

1819 The United States receives Florida from Spain as debt repayment.

1835 The Seminole lose the 2nd Seminole Indian War and are forced from the region.

1842 The Armed Occupation Act boosts white settlement of Central Florida.

1843 Orlando is established. Florida becomes a state two years later.

1850s Citrus groves are established. They, along with cattle, form the staple industries.

1856 Orlando becomes the county seat of Orange County.

1870 The St. John's River—from Jacksonville down through central Florida to Orlando—is the busiest waterway south of the Hudson. Orlando becomes a major marketplace and shipment point.

1882 The South Florida Railroad reaches Orlando and trade booms.

1913 Sanford splits from Orlando to become capital of Seminole County.

Post-war Orlando's aerospace industry boasts Cape Canaveral Space Center.

1966 Walt Disney buys 27,000 acres (10,925ha) of land to the southwest of the city for his vision: Walt Disney World®.

Dec 1966 Death of Walt Disney.

1971 Magic Kingdom® opens, followed by SeaWorld in 1973.

1990 Universal Studios® opens.

1998 Animal Kingdom joins the theme parks at Walt Disney World® Resort.

2010 The Wizarding World of Harry Potter opens at Universal Studios Islands of Adventure.

2013 Disney announces plans for a new "land" at Animal Kingdom based on the blockbuster *Avatar*.

THE BIG FREEZE

Winter had been progressing as normal when temperatures suddenly dropped to 24°F (-4°C) on December 27, 1894. The whole citrus crop of the state withered on the branch. The weather returned to normal in January but worse was to come. On February 9, 1895, temperatures plummeted to 17°F (-8°C), killing the trees that were the backbone of the industry. It took until 1912 for the citrus groves to recover.

Index

Orlando 25 Best

WRITTEN AND UPDATED BY Lindsay Bennett
SERIES EDITOR Clare Ashton
COVER DESIGN Chie Ushio, Yuko Inagaki
DESIGN WORK Tracey Freestone
IMAGE RETOUCHING AND REPRO Ian Little

Published in the United Kingdom by AA Publishing

ISBN 978-0-8041-4343-1

FIRST EDITION

All details in this book are based on information supplied to us at press time. Always confirm information when it matters, especially if you're making a detour to visit a specific place. Fodor's expressly disclaims any liability, loss, or risk, personal or otherwise, that is incurred as a consequence of the use of any of the contents of this book.

SPECIAL SALES
This book is available for special discounts for bulk purchases for sales promotions or premiums. For more information, email specialmarkets@randomhouse.com.

Color separation by AA Digital Department
Printed and bound by Leo Paper Products, China

10 9 8 7 6 5 4 3 2 1

A05141
Maps in this title produced from map data supplied by Global Mapping, Brackley, UK. © Global Mapping
Transport map © Communicarta Ltd, UK

The Automobile Association would like to thank the following photographers, companies and picture libraries for their assistance in the preparation of this book.

Abbreviations for the picture credits are as follows – (t) top; (b) bottom; (c) center; (l) left; (r) right; (AA) AA World Travel Library.

1 AA/T Souter; 2 AA/P Bennett; 3 AA/P Bennett; 4t AA/P Bennett; 4c AA/P Bennett; 5t AA/P Bennett; 5c Courtesy of Disney; 6t AA/P Bennett; 6cl Courtesy of Disney; 6cr Courtesy of Disney; 6bl Courtesy of Disney; 6blc Courtesy of Disney; 6brc Courtesy of Disney; 6br Courtesy of Disney; 7t AA/P Bennett; 7cl Courtesy of Universal Studios; 7cr Courtesy of Universal Studios; 7bl Courtesy of Universal Studios; 7br Courtesy of Universal Studios; 8 AA/P Bennett; 9 AA/P Bennett; 10t AA/P Bennett; 10ct AA/P Bennett; 10c AA/C Sawyer; 10/11cb AA/P Bennett; 10/11b AA/P Bennett; 11t AA/P Bennett; 11ct AA/P Bennett; 11c AA/P Bennett; 12 AA/P Bennett; 13i AA/P Bennett; 13ii AA/P Bennett; 13iii AA/P Bennett; 13iv AA/P Bennett; 13v AA/P Bennett; 13vi AA/P Bennett; 14i AA/P Bennett; 14ii AA/P Bennett; 14iii AA/P Bennett; 14iv AA/P Bennett; 14v AA/P Bennett; 14vi AA/T Souter; 15 AA/P Bennett; 16t AA/P Bennett; 16ct Imagestate; 16c Courtesy of Universal Studios; 16cb Courtesy of Boggy Creek Airboat Rides; 16b AA/P Bennett; 17t AA/P Bennett; 17ct Courtesy of Disney; 17c AA/P Bennett; 17cb AA/C Sawyer; 17b AA/P Bennett; 18t AA/P Bennett; 18cb AA/P Bennett; 18c AA/P Bennett; 18cb AA/P Bennett; 18b AA/P Bennett; 19t Courtesy of Disney; 19ct Courtesy of Universal Studios; 19c AA/P Bennett; 19cb Courtesy of Orlando Science Center; 19b Courtesy of Boggy Creek Airboat Rides; 20/21 Courtesy of Disney; 24l Courtesy of Disney; 24t Courtesy of Disney; 25 Courtesy of Disney; 26l AA/P Bennett; 26r AA/P Bennett; 27l Courtesy of Cirque du Soleil ®; 27r Courtesy of Lego; 28t Courtesy of Disney; 28/29t Courtesy of Disney; 28/29b Courtesy of Disney; 29r Courtesy of Disney; 30l Courtesy of Disney; 30/31t Courtesy of Disney; 30/31b Courtesy of Disney; 31 Courtesy of Disney; 32l Courtesy of Disney; 32/33t Courtesy of Disney; 32/33b Courtesy of Disney; 33t Courtesy of Disney; 34l AA/P Bennett; 34r AA/P Bennett; 35l Courtesy of Disney; 35r Courtesy of Disney; 36t Courtesy of Universal Studios; 36bl Courtesy of Disney; 36br Courtesy of Disney; 37t Courtesy of Universal Studios; 37b Courtesy of Disney; 38t Courtesy of Universal Studios; 38bl Courtesy of Disney; 38br Courtesy of Disney; 39t Courtesy of Universal Studios; 39bl Courtesy of Disney; 39br Courtesy of Disney; 40 Photodisc; 41 Courtesy of Disney; 42 AA/P Bennett; 43 AA/J Tims; 44 AA/J Tims; 45 Courtesy of Universal Studios; 48l AA/P Bennett; 48tr AA/P Bennett; 48/49 AA/P Bennett; 49t AA/P Bennett; 49cl AA/P Bennett; 50/51t Courtesy of Universal Studios; 50cl AA/P Bennett; 50c Courtesy of Universal Studios; 51cl AA/P Bennett; 51r AA/P Bennett; 52 Courtesy of Universal Studios; 53l Courtesy of Universal Studios; 53r AA/P Bennett; 54t Courtesy of Universal Studios; 54bl AA/P Bennett; 54br Courtesy of Universal Studios; 55t Courtesy of Universal Studios; 55bl Courtesy of Universal Studios; 55br Courtesy of Universal Studios; 56 AA/C Sawyer; 57 AA/P Bennett; 58 AA/J Tims; 59 AA/P Bennett; 62l AA/P Bennett; 62c AA/P Bennett; 62r AA/P Bennett; 63l AA/C Sawyer; 63r AA/P Bennett; 64l AA/P Bennett; 64tr AA/P Bennett; 64cr AA/P Bennett; 65tl AA/P Bennett; 65tr Courtesy of SeaWorld Adventure Park; 65bl AA/P Bennett; 65br Courtesy of SeaWorld Adventure Park; 66l AA/P Bennett; 66c AA/P Bennett; 66r AA/P Bennett; 67 AA/T Souter; 68t Courtesy of Universal Studios; 68bl AA/P Bennett; 68br Courtesy of Aquatica, SeaWorld Water Park; 69t Courtesy of Universal Studios; 69b AA/P Bennett; 70 AA/C Sawyer; 71 AA/C Sawyer; 72 AA/P Bennett; 73 AA/J Tims; 74 AA/J Tims; 75 Courtesy of Orlando Science Center; 78l Courtesy of Leu Gardens; 78c Courtesy of Leu Gardens; 78r Courtesy of Leu Gardens; 79l AA/P Bennett; 79c AA/P Bennett; 79r AA/P Bennett; 80 AA/P Bennett; 81l AA/P Bennett; 81r Courtesy of Orlando Science Center; 82l AA/P Bennett; 82r AA/P Bennett; 83t Courtesy of Universal Studios; 83b AA/P Bennett; 84 AA/P Bennett; 85 AA/T Souter; 86 AA/C Sawyer; 87 AA/P Bennett; 88 AA/J Tims; 89 AA/T Souter; 92l Courtesy of Boggy Creek Airboat Rides; 92r Courtesy of Boggy Creek Airboat Rides; 93l AA/P Bennett; 93c AA/P Bennett; 93r AA/P Bennett; 94l AA/P Bennett; 94r AA/P Bennett; 95l AA/P Bennett; 95r AA/T Souter; 96t Courtesy of Universal Studios; 96bl ; 96br AA/P Bennett; 97t Courtesy of Universal Studios; 97bl AA/P Bennett; 97br AA/P Bennett; 98t Courtesy of Busch Gardens Tampa; 98bl Courtesy of Busch Gardens Tampa; 98br Courtesy of Busch Gardens Tampa; 99t Courtesy of Busch Gardens Tampa; 99b Courtesy of Busch Gardens Tampa; 100t Courtesy of Busch Gardens Tampa; 100b Courtesy of Legoland Florida; 101t Courtesy of Busch Gardens Tampa; 101bl Courtesy of Legoland Florida; 101br Courtesy of Legoland Florida; 102t Courtesy of Busch Gardens Tampa; 102bl AA/P Bennett; 102br AA/P Bennett; 103t Courtesy of Busch Gardens Tampa; 103b AA/P Bennett; 104 AA/P Bennett; 105 AA/C Sawyer; 106t AA/P Bennett; 106c AA/J Tims; 107 AA/C Sawyer; 108t AA/C Sawyer; 108ct Photodisc; 108c Photodisc; 108cb AA/C Sawyer; 108b Photodisc; 109 AA/C Sawyer; 110 AA/C Sawyer; 111 AA/C Sawyer; 112 AA/C Sawyer; 113 AA/P Bennett; 114 AA/P Bennett; 115 AA/P Bennett; 116 AA/P Bennett; 117 AA/P Bennett; 118 AA/P Bennett; 119 AA/P Bennett; 120 AA/P Bennett; 121 AA/P Bennett; 122 AA/P Bennett; 123 AA/P Bennett; 124t AA/P Bennett; 124bl AA/P Bennett; 124bc AA/P Bennett; 124/125b Courtesy of Universal Studios; 125t AA/P Bennett; 125bc AA/J Davison; 125br AA/M Chaplow

Every effort has been made to trace the copyright holders, and we apologize in advance for any accidental errors. We would be happy to apply the corrections in the following edition of this publication.